Fetal Alcohol

By

Mom Irene

authorHOUSE

1663 LIBERTY DRIVE, SUITE 200
BLOOMINGTON, INDIANA 47403
(800) 839-8640
www.authorhouse.com

First published by AuthorHouse 03/31/04

ISBN: 1-4184-0563-9 (e)
ISBN: 1-4184-0564-7(sc)

Printed in the United States of America
Bloomington, IN

This book is printed on acid free paper.

About the Author

"Mom Irene", as she has chosen to be identified, was born and raised in the upper Midwest during the "great depression" years. She grew up in a rural home where material wealth was scarce and hard work was plentiful. She learned very early in life the value of a loving family, and was instilled with Christian morals. Irene received unconditional love from her family, and passed the same on to each of her children, whether biological or adopted.

Irene has been a very talented and respected author/poet throughout her life. She has written and published countless poems, several books and numerous major magazine articles. After raising her four biological sons, Irene and her husband set forth on a life journey that found them adopting and raising eight children with disabilities. Two of these children suffered from Fetal Alcohol Syndrome, which is the focus of this book.

Irene has become an outspoken advocate for those persons who were dealt mental and physical challenges through no fault of their own. She is consulted by doctors and other "professionals" who learn from her experience and knowledge and use it to help their clients. Irene and her husband are remarkable people with uncommon selflessness. They are both true heroes.

Mike (Irene's son)

Dedication

This book is dedicated to two very brave and courageous young men who struggle daily with Fetal Alcohol Syndrome, my sons, Ben and Jon. Also, to my husband who is a great father and who works with me as a "team", for without his love, help and patience, I could never have gotten through our son's tough times. I also want to thank my son, Mike, for all the help he has given me to get this book ready for the printer, and for his encouragement and belief in what I am doing. Also, to Jo Ann and to Jan H. and to Dianne, who have also walked this path and to all others who have or will in the future. We are parents of twelve, eight of whom are adopted with special needs. We are also grandparents and great grandparents. I have changed my name and the names of my two sons, for privacy reasons.

Mom Irene

PRELUDE

Many professionals have written about Fetal Alcohol Syndrome (F.A.S.) and Fetal Alcohol Effect (F.A.E.). I am not a professional, and do not claim to be. But, as a very concerned mother, I believe that common sense is the number one quality needed to parent any child, along with patience, a sense of humor, and a Christian home where children are taught good morals and about the Lord.

I am the mother of six sons and six daughters. Two of these sons were adopted after the four biological sons were grown and left home. Both of these adopted sons have F.A.S. The older son, now age 29, is of Native American heritage, and came to us at age 7 years, 5 months. He is the least affected behaviorally.

The younger son (Caucasian) is now 24 years old and came to us on his 5th birthday. Each son is very different, but both have a common denominator – they are brain damaged forever, caused by nine months before birth when their biological mothers consumed alcohol. My understanding is that both were binge drinkers, one at adolescence.

It seems ironic that 9 months of these 2 sons' lives could affect a full lifetime, even 90 years or more. My desire is that there will be more education of young people in the homes and schools that they may understand what alcohol use during these 9 months (and sometimes before pregnancy occurs) can cause to a human life. Sometimes, there are several generations of F.A.S. / F.A.E. The cycle needs to be broken. There needs to be intervention to stop it. I personally believe that in many of these cases, it may take incarceration during pregnancy.

My connection to Ph.D. Robin La Due In Washington State has been a great help to me in parenting my two sons. Dr. Ten Bensel at the U. of MN was also of tremendous help. He was very knowledgeable about F.A.S. / F.A.E. and very sympathetic to our many concerns on what to do. People like this mean so much to parents, as most of us need their encouragement. A kind, understanding word can keep us going. We have met both these kind, caring professionals and the kind who only criticize. We, the parents and other caregivers, have a tremendous job and unless one has lived it, they can never know. Walk in our shoes a mile, then you will know.

We chose this path, although we did not understand it all at the time. Having parented other children with disabilities previously, we expected it to be similar. However, it is very different. F.A.S. kids march to a different drummer.

Through nearly fifty years of child rearing, I have had many experiences, many observations, and I'm sure I've made mistakes. It is a very rewarding feeling to hear a child say, "I love you", or give you a big hug. What more could anyone want from life?

When I was in high school, I worked in a local grocery store. There was a young man, older than I was, who also worked there who probably had a severe form of Cerebral Palsy. Walking and talking were difficult for him. He was carrying boxes of fruits and vegetables up a stairway, opening them and other such jobs. Even for the 50 cents he got a week that he spent on candy for his Mom's gift, I felt he was being used. But, even worse in my eyes was that he was being tantalized and laughed at by people who should have been intelligent enough to know better. I became very angry until my blood felt hot in my body and I lashed out at them to their shock, I'm sure.

There have been a few times much later than those years, when my two sons with F.A.S. have been unaware that the remarks made about them were much the same as I had heard those years ago when I was young. Yet, my sons thought that these cruel people were being friendly and called them "friends". There is no place for cruel people in our society. They actually nauseate me. Even ignorance is not this horrible. Ignorant people do not know any better.

There is one thing that I will not tolerate – that is if anyone teases or humiliates our sons. This is cruel and hurtful. There have been a few instances during their school years and afterwards that this has happened. Our sons have reported to us and we have taken care of it. If it is someone who has a supervisor or parent, we go to the source and as far as we know, that ends it.

It was from that time on, that I felt a need to advocate for those who could not do so for themselves. Perhaps I could say it has been my "calling" in life. The Lord has given me many such opportunities. At these times, perhaps, he was preparing me for what was to lie ahead when we became parents of eight children with special needs, two of these are who I write about in the pages ahead.

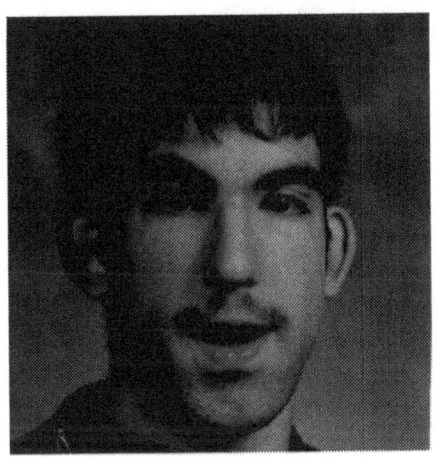

Jon (present day)

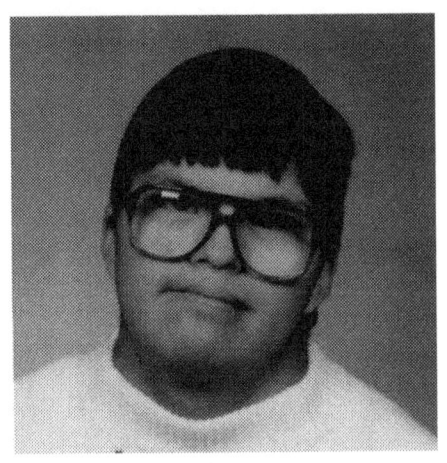

Ben (present day)

Table of Contents

Chapter 1
The Nightmare

The dream seemed so real! "Mommy...Mommy", my seventeen year old son cried as he was being led by a policeman to a small room; gleaming white walls surrounding a table with several sets of straps over white sheets. It was an electric chair. I was walking fast behind him sobbing and helpless. "Mommy, don't let them kill me", he pleaded, glancing back at me with terrified eyes. That frightened look brought a chill to my body as tears streamed down my cheeks. My son in a man's body with a child's mind, wracked with all the abnormalities inwardly and outwardly, the results of prenatal alcohol on his tiny developing brain.

I jumped out of bed, sweating profusely with a heartbeat as loud and as fast as a tractor's motor! In the dream, I didn't know exactly what he had done to bring him to this terrible place. But, I knew that it must have been very serious, very severe, and I, his mother, never felt more helpless than this during my entire life. In reality, he had been in court that day for throwing a piece of concrete and hitting a female staff at the group home where he resided and she had filed charges against him. I do not believe that staff should file charges for when they are hired working in homes as my son's home, they are aware of the fact that these incidents are a possibility.

Although our son was on high doses of psychotropic drugs to help him control his behaviors, he continued to have very little impulse control. He also was always very remorseful after he had hurt anyone. He had been evaluated at a large hospital at puberty when his behaviors escalated immensely.

This nightmare still haunts me every time the phone rings. It haunts me in my sleep as well. It haunts me in every dream I dream about him. I always fear that my son, adopted at the age of five years, will someday do something so serious that my nightmare could become a reality. This happened over seven years ago. It seems like it was yesterday.

What is so very tragic is that he is a very special, caring and loving young man. He is compassionate and deeply feels empathy for others. He has an acting talent and a very unique sense of humor. He can make you laugh when you feel like crying. He would give you everything he owns if you would ask for it. He always has a kind word for those who are grieving or sick or depressed. He is a wonderful person.

It's only those times when he loses control that are scary. These times aren't frequent, but they are not predictable. One never knows when or where they may happen. They have happened in all environments and in no set pattern. He's like a Jekyl and Hyde. He is my son, no matter what the future brings.

Jon asks me often, "Mom. What will happen to me when you die? Who will love me then?" All I can answer is that he'll always be in my heart, wherever I am, even when I die. And he will. He is my son.

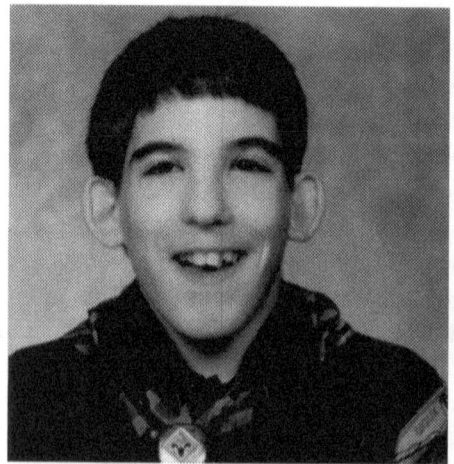

Jon the Cub Scout   Jon the clown

Chapter 2

Ben's Arrival

On a warm March day in 1980, we traveled to South Dakota to visit a seven-year-old boy of Sioux Indian heritage who had been diagnosed with Down Syndrome. Our hope was to adopt another boy to add to our already adopted two sets of twin girls with Down Syndrome. When we learned that he had already lived in six homes, it seemed strange. After all, children with Down Syndrome are very sweet and loving children and we enjoyed parenting them. We first met Ben at a school he attended and we immediately fell in love with him. We learned from his social worker that he had lived with his birth mother the first year of his life, but that he was hospitalized at about 5 months of age. He had then been diagnosed as a "failure to thrive" baby. This was attributed to his Down Syndrome. We learned little of his previous placements after the mother relinquished him, except that for three years he had lived in another state with a family who had planned to adopt him but after three years decided that they couldn't love him, so they sent him back to South Dakota. We took this very insecure boy home with us to Minnesota and we hung his picture on the wall beside of our other children's pictures. Every day when he came home from school, he looked on the wall to see if his picture was still there. We later learned that the previous home where he had lived also had his picture on the wall, but the people took it down and sent it with him when he moved. So, as long as his picture was on our wall, Ben figured he was also still in our home.

From the very first time I saw Ben, I knew that he must have something more than Down Syndrome. There was something very different about him than others with D.S. Perhaps, we thought it was the result of having seven homes in the first seven years of his life. He was a good, loving child, always giving hugs and wanting to "help" with whatever we were doing. In time, he even quit looking for his picture on the wall.

After Ben had adjusted, we adopted a nine-month old girl, also with D.S. Ben loved her from the start and has always been protective of her. Later, we felt that he would like to have a brother, rather than be the only boy at home. Although we already had four grown sons (mine biologically), they no longer lived at home, so Ben didn't have a lot of interaction with them.

Ben on the way home

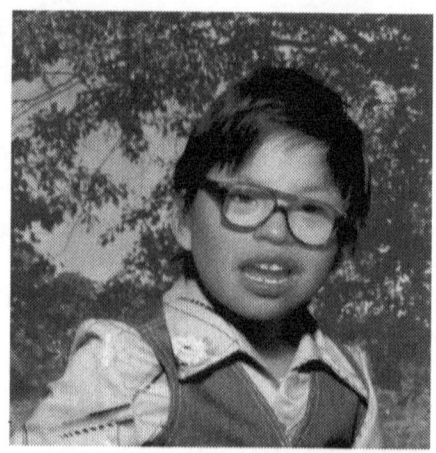

Ben (7 yrs old) a week later

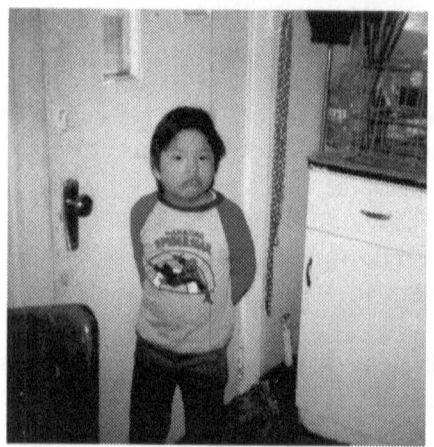

Ben at NaNa's 1st visit

Ben with puppets

Chapter 3
Jon Arrives

It was November 1983 on his fifth birthday that Jon arrived. I traveled to a western state to meet him. His worker took me to his Montessori School to meet him. He was so tiny and thin and his head was tilted to one side. I bent down to greet him and he looked straight up at me and in a soft pixie-like voice that matched his pixie-like appearance, he asked, "who are you?" I replied, "I'm Mommy." "Oh", he said rather slowly and more like a question, "two Mommies", of course (foster Mom and I).

His worker explained that the home he was in was his third home and that his psychological read that he needed a placement permanently, and soon if he was ever to bond to a family. She also said that he had Fetal Alcohol Syndrome and was mentally handicapped.

After a few days of getting acquainted with this little boy, I went home. The agency said I should go home and decide if we wanted to adopt him. Of course we did! From the very first, there were no doubts in our minds. The paperwork was complete and his social worker flew with him to our state so he could be home by his fifth birthday. This tiny, very hyperactive little boy came in to our hearts and home and from the very moment he arrived, and until the day we die, he changed our lives forever!

Both Jon's extreme hyperactivity and lack of impulse control made it difficult for everyone who worked with him and for himself most of all. He was very humorous and at school he was the class clown. At first, when he arrived home he stiffened out when I would try to hold him. Then, he got sick one day and he crawled on my lap and cuddled up and let me hold and rock him. From that moment on, he bonded to me.

Discipline that worked for children with D.S. seemed not to work with Jon. He needed much structure in his life. From the beginning, he would spin in a unique pattern wearing his headset and playing his beloved "country music". In his bedroom, he would lie down and rock side to side. He climbed across the ceiling beam with his long feet and webbed long thin fingers, much to my fear that he would get hurt. He never did. Even his mind seemed "hyped up!" His responses were quicker than lightning at times.

Although his psychological testing gave him an IQ of around 50, we felt this was much too low. People thought sometimes that he was intelligent, but in reality he grasped at bits and pieces of conversations, TV, etc., and came up with some very interesting expressive language. One day when Jon and I went shopping, our car stalled on the railroad tracks. I said out-loud to myself, "what will I do? The engine died." Jon replied, "well, bury it then!"

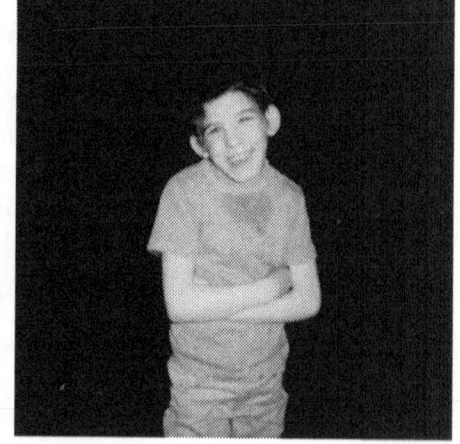

Jon (5 yrs old)   Jon's sweet smile

Chapter 4
Comparisons

During those first years after Jon came to be our son, I saw vague similarities to Ben. I researched Fetal Alcohol Syndrome and all I could read on it, as well as attending workshops. I talked to doctors, Psychologists, Psychiatrists, Pediatricians, Teachers, and parents of other children with F.A.S. I inhaled all I could on the condition. It was all very interesting, but living with someone with this condition was unlike, yet similar to any of the things I read of or heard of. I kept in the back of my mind the question, "could Ben have F.A.S.?" One day, I called the agency he was registered with and talked to a lady there. I asked if Ben could possibly have F.A.S., as well as D.S. He answer was no surprise. She told me that she couldn't give me a professional answer, but that she could give me her opinion as she knew the birth mother. So, he was!! Later, I asked a doctor who told me he had thought this right along, but he just hadn't said anything. Another chromosome study proved that he does have D.S. as well.

Until Jon arrived, I couldn't put my finger on what was so different about Ben than most children with D.S. He had a double diagnosis. I did see that his ears had looked like those of children who had F.A.S. in one of the photos I'd seen. Also, he had a long smooth area (philtrum) between his nose and upper lip. He also lost everything and took things from his sisters, such as their music cassettes. He seemed not to understand the connection between behavior and consequences.

Ben enjoys train

7

Chapter 5

Just Brothers

Both boys had a good relationship, although their personalities are very different. They enjoyed being in each other's company and had a special concern for one another. Jon has always been hyperactive. Ben is not. Jon has been violent at times. Ben is not. Although Jon is a thin, short man, he can be very strong. His dreams have been to become a country singer, to sing with Pam Tillis, who he has met and had his picture taken with. Ben enjoys Pow-Wows and dances, fishing, biking, and the out of doors.

Their dreams are not for the future, but for the immediate moment. When Ben was a little boy, he would put out his arms as if to fly. I called him "little bird". He also led me to the window to see the moon, which has always fascinated him. He strove for acceptance, and his worker called him a "survivor", as he had known rejection. Seven homes in his first seven years of life left him insecure, which took a long time to overcome. He had also known malnutrition, so he hid food in his pockets for awhile. Mashed potatoes, meat and vegetables were even stuffed away. Being hungry, moving from place to place, never really knowing "home" as others do certainly took its toll. At this writing, Ben has been our son for 22 years. He's been a joy to parent and I've learned a lot from him about how important it is for a child to know he belongs in a family. Rejection must be very hard on the young and helpless and for those like himself, who do not understand why. He could give love. Why couldn't he be loved?

Brothers bonding

Brothers with Santa

Pow-Wow Ben went to

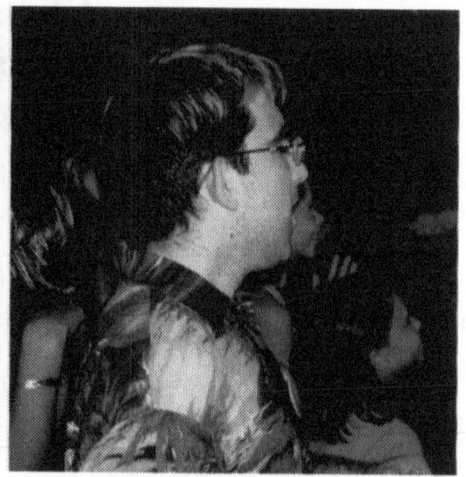

Jon at concert

Ben and sister by Tee Pee

Jon with Country Star

Brotherly love

Brothers at play

Chapter 6
The Diagnosis

There is so much F.A.S. – F.A.E. F.A.E. are Fetal Alcohol Effects without the characteristic "look" that I call "Elf-like", or "Pixie-like" that are associated with people who have the full "syndrome" (F.A.S.). These conditions are 100% preventable. They are also 100% incurable because it is damage to the brain. This is also a condition that is very often left undiagnosed, perhaps more often misdiagnosed.

Many of these children are in numerous foster care placements. Others are adopted or raised by grandparents or other relatives. Some birth mothers struggle with their addiction and still raise their alcohol-affected child or children. These mothers are a different story. All that I mean to make known here is how two very different young men in their twenties have a common denominator and that denominator is a brain injured by alcohol use of the mother. Why? Why? Why?

Often times I read or hear of all the damage that alcohol can do to families, such as child neglect, abuse, drunk driving that may kill innocent people on the highways. As I look at these articles I seldom hear of the innocent babies born to a life (sometimes a long life) with insurmountable problems, a few of which may be seizures, heart problems, eye problems, ear problems, having no concept of time or place or space. Their lack of impulse control causes behavioral problems, often violence. Many are also mentally handicapped. The people with the "effects" only, often "fall between the cracks", because they do not look different and they can sound better than they really are knowledgeable. Some are very verbal, as our sons are.

Chapter 7
Trying To Understand

So many times still my nightmare reoccurs to haunt me. I know that Jon is capable of doing great harm not because he wants to, not because he plans to, but because his brain does not always "connect". The blank spaces in a much smaller than normal brain do not "keep it all together".

There seem to be no real answers as long as pregnant women choose to use alcoholic beverages. There are no cures for the innocent babies born to them. For we parents who adopt or foster them, we do our best to parent them wisely and lovingly. To give them the normalcy of real family life, while inwardly we know the reality of their futures. For those who teach them, there is a challenge as none other. While patience and understanding are much needed qualities for all who play a part in their lives, we must find out how they learn and accept what they cannot learn. Many of these children seem to be lost at about fourth grad level.

For the doctors who still sometimes tell a pregnant patient that a few drinks won't hurt her baby, they should be saying that she is playing Russian Roulette with her baby's brain, each drink she takes. In my opinion, every bar should be having signs up that say, "we do not serve alcoholic beverages to pregnant women". If only one child could be spared from suffering the effects of this disability, it would be well worthwhile.

I have personally over the past twenty-two years, witnessed first hand the heartaches, the struggles, the pain that these children and young adults live with and for myself, the same heartaches, struggles and pain. Love alone cannot erase it.

Chapter 8
Help

It concerns me when my young men want to go to the toy department in the stores, instead of looking at automobiles or going on dates. Their future doesn't include college or marriage or children, or cars. It concerns me when they go to court for doing things they could not control and have no understanding of. They do not understand right or wrong or why consequences occur or what the justice system is all about. It concerns me deeply that others may look at them and hear them talk and not understand that their brain cannot comprehend these things. It frightens me to think that my nightmare could very well become reality. My heart bleeds at the very thought.

What can we do for children and young folks with F.A.S.? My answer is to build a ring of protection around them according to their needs. For I have learned that love is not enough for them, but like little children they need protection and structure. That they are unable to live life without this basic need to keep them safe from others and others safe from them. These children need early identification, early intervention, understanding and patient teachers and caregivers. Because they usually do not learn right from wrong by logical consequences as others would, the ring of protection must be strong around them. Judges and lawyers and others need to remember that it is not willingly that they lose control or act inappropriately, but rather that they have brain damage. They are as vulnerable as little children all of their lives. Society needs to be aware of their vulnerabilities, no matter what their ages.

Our sons, because of obvious mental retardation, have been under supervision while some with higher IQ's have not. Yet, they too may have no social skills and may make poor choices. Thus they may be held more accountable for their behaviors. With early identification, this ring of protection can prevent many problems during their school years and on in to adulthood.

Ben at summer camp with Counselor

Ben with a very good friend

Chapter 9

Medications

I believe that some psychotropic medications are of help in some cases. I also know that other diagnoses are common along with F.A.S. & F.A.E. There is, however, no cure for F.A.S. or F.A.E. Only prevention of maternal drinking during pregnancy is the answer.

For parents or other caregivers of this population, I suggest you keep a good sense of humor and a loving heart that understands that these people are unique individuals, not to be stereotyped, yet one realizes there are likenesses. The common denominator is that they are brain damaged. They act on impulse and don't seem to "connect" in understanding consequences. They are very challenging to parent and to work with, but knowing them can be one of the most rewarding experiences that one can encounter in life. Two of these young men are my sons, and through all the challenges and heartaches, I am proud to be their mother. When times get difficult (and they certainly do), I try to remember what the Pediatrician who first saw Jon when he was five years old said after watching him for awhile, "and he can't help it." To me, that sums up all I could say in this book.

Jon on slide

Chapter 10

The Justice System

My fear is that many in the justice system do not fully understand that people with F.A.S. or F.A.E. have a condition caused by brain damage. Some of these people are very verbal, although they sound very much like they comprehend, this often is not reality. I can recall so many examples.

One son wanted to sell his old computer for the same price as the new elaborate computer he wanted. Money is something he just doesn't understand. He told me once that something cost $25,000. I asked if he knew how much that was and he looked up at me questioning, "twenty cents?" When a staff member took him to court because he assaulted her, he told me, "Mom, the only way we can settle this is if I sue her." When asked what a Judge is for, he answered, "to put me in jail." Yet, in many ways when he converses one would think he was quite normal. He is 24 years old. Neither son will ever drive a car, nor will they go anywhere alone without someone to guide them.

Someone will always have to take charge of their finances and see that they take baths, shampoo their hair, and wear clean clothing, which is appropriate for the season. Someone will always need to see that some vulture doesn't take advantage of them and they will always need guardians to advocate for their rights and their best interest. In these ways, I feel they are more fortunate than the thousands who every day fall into a population who have no one to help them throughout their lives because their IQ's may be higher. Yet, they have the same problems socially and therefore are totally held accountable for what they do. Most are the people who were never diagnosed or probably misdiagnosed. I see this population every now and then, and my heart bleeds for them. Some may end up going through life, sliding along where others may end up in prisons or worse yet, as my nightmare.

Chapter 11
The Caregiver

From personal experience, I can truthfully say that having a child with F.A.S. / F.A.E. in your home changes your life forever. There are challenges and there are rewards. Had I never had a child with this disability, I would have missed out on both sides of the coin. I would say they have balanced out. It took a lot of patience to keep up with the hyperactivity one of the boys had. He was never still, and many early mornings, he was up in his room, for night and day were all the same to him.

The caregiver needs understanding from others, not criticism. They need to educate others in their child's life about their unique, brain damaged child and how he "processes" best, what forms of discipline (if any) have worked, what meds (if any) the child takes, and when and how much. Caregivers need to learn all they can about the condition, although actual experience is something that one needs to really understand this condition.

When Jon began puberty at age eleven, he suddenly (seemed like overnight) go more than excessive leg hair and his severe behavioral outbursts began. We asked the school Superintendent to obtain the help of a behavioral analyst to help them and ourselves to help Jon control his behavior, because none of us (school or home) had had much success. Measures used with other kids seemed to fail. The behavioral analyst came up with some strategies, but most also failed.

When Jon was fifteen, we took him to the University of Minnesota to meet with Dr. Ten Bensel who was a wonderful caring person who helped us to deal with the crisis of this time. He referred us to a Psychiatrist who put Jon on medications. At the time, they were Lithium and Tegretol. In later years, Tegretol was dropped and other meds have been used, including Paxil and Resperidol.

We kept Jon home until he was 15 ½ years of age. We then admitted him to a group facility because of his threats to his sisters and sexual innuendoes. The group facility was made up of 15 individuals with various degrees of M.R. It was not ideal, we felt, as Jon was unlike the others in many ways. However, he was only within 20 miles of our home, so we could see him often. He was very attached to our family, and us to him, so we had no choice if we were to keep our closeness. In our rural community, there just aren't choices of residential facilities. The administration was very accepting of him, and they worked well with us to provide appropriate services that would enhance Jon's interests and his unique needs.

Jon put on plays to entertain the others, staff as well. He wrote us letters and visited us at home. He went shopping, to bingo, biking, swimming, and to movies. A friend of our family took him out to eat, camping and to concerts when she was working with Ben. One time I sent Jon with her to Nashville, Tennessee to go to Country Music concerts and to see what the music industry was all about. This was his dream come true, a long lasting highlight in his life.

Jon dressed up for Halloween

Ben's dream was a trip to the Black Hills of South Dakota. There, he was able to visit places that enhanced his beautiful Sioux heritage.

Jon came home for a few weeks after he had lived at the group home, but this didn't work out so he went back to the group home. It was much better when the agency bought homes in the town with four clients rather than fifteen. It was less stimulating for Jon and was more of a home like atmosphere. He still works at a D.A.C. in the city where he lives. He still believes that if he could move, the grass would be greener somewhere else. He believes he should be independent, but all that know him know that that is not reality. We are content to know that Jon is protected in his environment at present. Staff works with him on activities of daily living and other needs. He comes home for Sunday suppers and takes part in some other family parties, etc. He was diagnosed at birth with F.A.S. and he knows this. He knows he is adopted also. He has "full-blown" F.A.S., which Ben does not.

Ben gets along at home well. He has fewer needs. He enjoys his Dad and going fishing, to POW-Wows, bowling, camping, and going out to eat. Eating is his greatest pleasure, and he loves choosing where he wants to eat, when he goes out. He talks about his birthday all year long. He is slightly interested in girls, and has a friend with the same diagnosis of F.A.S. who he says is his girlfriend. He sees her occasionally at dances and they do enjoy each other's company.

Ben at dance with friend

Ben at dance

Jon likes a certain type of girl (blonde) and insists she not have a disability. He tends to call certain selected staff (and teacher's assistants – when in school) his "dates" when they work with him. This comes in spurts of his life. He gets fixated on different areas (something he wants, someone he wants, somewhere he wants to live). These phases come and eventually pass, but sometimes with much anger.

Jon and Ben both enjoy giving cards, etc., for birthdays, anniversaries, weddings, Father's and Mother's Days, etc. Both are sensitive and can tell whether a person likes them, respects them and "hears" them. Every person needs these basics. Everyone deserves them. Low self-esteem results when these are lacking.

When our sons moving days arrived, I don't know how any words can explain my feelings, except that grief would be the closest word. I know my heart sunk because of various reasons. The thoughts haunted me day and night. Not only did they have to adjust, I also had to. Would they be happy in their new environment? Would their staff understand them and their needs? Would they really care? Would they get their medications on time? How would they handle the one son's behavioral problems? This concern – this worry, and more raced through my mind for a long time. I wrote the following article:

Moving Day – May 1994

Our son, nearly 16 but going on 3, is moving today. The lump in my chest and the fought back tears in my eyes represent my deep love for him and the closeness we've shared since we adopted him on his 5th birthday.

I do not know if he (or I) can exist apart, for we have been glued together for so many years. We have battled this full-blown F.A.S. with many a long day (and some longer nights). We have tried together to educate the schools and community. We have visited doctors, counselors, psychiatrists and we have used medications which helped some.

He has learned to be a good swimmer, skater, horseback rider, bowler, snow-tuber and fisherman.

We have never overcome the impulsivity, hyperactivity or the myriad of socially unacceptable behaviors. We take one day at a time and this is the day we finally face, residential care.

My son asked me if I am dying and if that is why he is moving. He does not want to move. I am torn between what is best for him and the rest of our family. He does not understand that we need to do this for all of our sakes. The day has come as we have worried it would. It came so fast. He was a little boy only yesterday. Today, he is half man, half child. Our love will never be any less, nor will our involvement in his life.

I have packed his belongings – the guitar, the helmet for his bike, his clothing and his treasures. I have tried with all within me to explain "why" this day has come. I know he cannot comprehend it but I've tried so hard to make it as easy as possible for him.

I've told him it only takes a little while for us to go visit him or bring him home to visit, but he does not comprehend distance, or time or that the red car in a far-away town doesn't belong to an aunt and uncle, just because they also have a red car.

The group home isn't far, but it is an eternity when I walk by his empty room. He looks sad; I turn away so he cannot see my tears. He starts spinning around, something he has never done before. I ask him why he is spinning and he replies, "that is the way my world is going right now." I go toward him, arms open. He runs toward me and we hug. "I love you", I say with a shaking voice and trying to smile. He replies, "I know mom. What will happen to me if you die?" I say, "you would still live in my heart. You always will be in my heart, so carry that with you always." He looks at me wondering. The lump fills my throat.

Follow-Up Note Sept. 1994

Therapy for me will come in writing. He is having much difficulty in the group home. It isn't a perfect situation, but there are none in our area. If I had money, I would create a community he and others with F.A.S. / F.A.E. need. We have few resources.

In the first four months, he has been so aggressive and violent. He threw a piece of concrete at a staff member, which resulted in 4 stitches in the face and a cracked cheekbone. The police were called and he was taken to jail in handcuffs. He may go to court for assault. That day he was taken to the emergency room for a shot to calm him down. After many calls, he was hospitalized short term to balance medications.

I can't handle it well. What can I do to find the right place for him? He needs a smaller environment, totally protected, with less stimulation. Oh, how much my heartaches for him! My heartaches have been many, but my rewards are all in knowing him. The Lord truly blessed us when he let us parent this young boy.

We have had hundreds of meetings with the providers of service. Most of the time, we agreed and everything went quite smoothly. The provider was always willing to listen and understand our concerns. We appreciated, and still do, all that is done for Jon, still in his home away from home. We know it isn't always easy. I'm sure it never will be, but he is worth it all.

Our oldest son, Ben, lived in a facility for several years, but returned home and has done fine. He enjoys being in his stable environment again.

Both fellows graduated from high school with regular diplomas. This was quite an accomplishment for them. They did both learn to read, which I insisted on. It makes their world much more interesting. The most difficult for them to learn is math and social skills.

Jon wants a girl friend, but has no idea that he cannot just expect every girl he wants to go with him. This includes movie stars, country singers, and actors. Wanting and having wants become reality are all the same to him. But, when he gives up on one "want", he moves on to another for awhile and so on.

In order to do what we feel best for our special needs young people, we went to court before their 18th birthdays and obtained guardianship. This is not to control their lives, but rather to protect them and help them to make good choices. We know that someone will always need to see that their best interests are met. In many ways, they do not understand what is in their best interest. We need to explain to them, as best we can, the "whys". There is the team (us as guardians, our sons, a social worker and providers of services) who meet semi-annually or annually (in some situations) or more often (if needed) to discuss their progress, their meds (if any), their problems, and any other concerns we have or our son has.

He leads the meetings at these times. I'm sure this helps his self-esteem, which is so often low in this population, because they cannot always be in control of their lives. Parents or other caregivers and staff with guardians must make decisions that sometimes are not what the person himself would want, but what is for his best interest. Most of the time, this can be done tactfully and somewhat explained in a way the person who it affects could understand, enough anyway to be satisfied. Sometimes this is impossible and I feel badly for the son. Then I tell him that I love him and as his mom and dad, we need to do what will help him and he usually will reply with a, "Yea mom, I know, but". For me, that ends the conversation, as it will get nowhere except frustration and escalates until he may have a behavior. Ben will not argue very often and is much mellower, much easier to explain to so that he is satisfied with the final decision.

As for the biological mothers who abuse alcohol, I for one feel that there needs to be laws that it is a crime if a woman knows she is pregnant and still abuses alcohol. A mother by nature wants to protect her young before birth and after. It should be their choice either to stop drinking alcoholic beverages or be incarcerated until the baby is born; and after the child is born, have the choice of keeping the baby and raising it and stop drinking, or choosing to continue to drink and lose her child.

When a child is born with F.A.S. / F.A.E., it costs society a lot of money as there are many more medical and psychological issues that require, in many cases, monumental dollars throughout their lifetimes. In the school system, many of these children must have special education, more one on one help. Jon is legally blind. Both sons wear glasses. Jon also takes high does of psychotropic medications. Both sons need staff or parental supervision all of the time. Although our sons do not have heart problems or seizures, these health problems plague many others. Yet, the hugs, the smiles, the sense of humor, the compassion our sons have, make them a real blessing in our lives.

Through the heartaches have come real bonding, which many call rare in these people. Concern for others is certainly one of their characteristics that makes them dear to us. Remorse after behaviors is also a good quality our sons possess. The one problem that I would change, if I could, would be their poor (sometimes lacking completely) control over impulsiveness. Like a "temper tantrum" in a small child, it escalates to a point where it is out of control.

Chapter 12

Sweets

One night, at 2:00 A.M., I awoke to a loud giggling noise coming from one of our son's rooms. Going inside his room, I found him perched up on his dresser, like a chicken in a roost. "Hi mom", he said, still giggling loudly. "I'm drunk", was his next remark. Looking over his room, I found a large empty bag of those large sugar Easter Eggs that I had put away in the cupboard for the upcoming Easter Sunday Egg hunt. He had eaten them all! I called it a sugar drunk. Like an alcoholic on alcohol, he was reacting to the sugar. Some will disagree on sugar being capable of doing what alcohol could do. My son's early morning experience proved to me that sugar (at least that much sugar) caused him to have a different personality that time. I also had been noticing that he became more hyperactive when he had a lot of sweets. It seemed that he craved sweets as well.

Both sons with F.A.S. are similar in this respect. Any candy, cookie, cake or sweet sodas seem to affect them. We never gave them a lot of sweets, but rather saved them for birthdays and other special holidays.

Ben and Nephew

Chapter 13
Complex Behavior

There seems to be a slim line between a developmentally delayed person and a genius. At times, our sons have been both, which most people cannot understand. Unless one has known them very well, they would not necessarily understand what I mean. Being with them for so many years, it becomes easy.

Jon has an ability to predict what will happen, at times. It is something like E.S.P. The human brain is so complex. I sometimes see an overlapping of conditions, such as autism, in Ben. Not knowing either set of birth parents and knowing very little about them, it is also difficult to know what is genetic, what is their natural personality, and what is from the damage alcohol did to their brain. Sometimes, I've wondered how different they could have or would have been without the syndrome that has robbed them of so much, yet made them unique and precious in a way that only God can know. To our family, they are accepted unconditionally, and these "other personalities" have no place in their lives. What could have been is no longer and issue. We go on and cannot change the past.

There are many secondary conditions that occur often in people with this syndrome. I believe that I have seen the following, at one time or another in at least one son:

1. Attention Deficit Hyperactivity Disorder. Although both sons would easily be diagnosed with A.D.D., only one could be said to have A.D.H.D.
2. Autism. Rarely, but at times, both sons have exhibited symptoms of this condition.
3. Depression. In Jon, I suspect this condition, at times.
4. Bipolar. Jon's moods can, at times, fluctuate between highs and lows.

Do not think for a moment that there is nothing that can be done to help with children who have F.A.S. / F.A.E. Our sons had small rooms. Jon loved to "cocoon". He would wrap up tightly in a blanket on his mattress. It seemed that this was then "his quiet, secure place." He would roll on his bed, or on the floor. This was his "space" to unload a mind that was boggled with things he didn't process as others could. Provide structure; repeat – repeat – repeat. Be consistent. Routine is a great help. They need to know what comes next, even if they can tell time, they cannot "connect" time on a clock or a watch with "this is the time to get up, go to work, eat a meal, etc."

Jon couldn't sit still long enough to eat a meal. He would eat a bite, move around the room, and then come back to the table for more food. We would repeat each time; "this is the time we eat." Finally, after many repetitions, he decided that the food would be removed when everyone else had finished their meal. Sometimes, counseling may benefit the child or adult; however we found that to find a counselor who understands that your child is brain damaged while listening to the chattering child may be quite difficult. The counselors may feel the child or adult with F.A.S. / F.A.E. understands because he is so verbal, while this is not usually the case. Picking a counselor who has had enough experience working with this population is the "key" for success.

Jon excels in swimming. This is a great sport that uses a lot of his excessive energy. It also has built his self-esteem. He would, sometimes, be the only one in our local pool on cold days. Both sons love bowling, fishing, camping and biking; all wonderful ways to use up energy that leads to problems if they are bored. They need people around them who have a spot in their lives to provide encouragement and emotional support. In school, parents need to have life skills be the most important part of their day. Art is also a great way for many to describe what they feel. Some will make little "booklets" about their summer, or other subjects of interest to them.

Music, something soothing, can help them calm. Ignoring inappropriate behaviors as much as possible is a good approach as well as praising others who have appropriate behaviors. Try to redirect a behavior – try to catch them when they do well and praise. Because a morning can be so busy, we always had everything ready the night before. They were also put in the same place each time to try and model that articles all have their place.

Jon wrote, "We went to the high school to watch a show. The show was <u>DRUGS</u>. It was loud, but it was nice. Over 2 billion people was there. I like the show. I thought of my future and I'm not going to smoke and that something to think about, and I will have a better life."

Jon at High School Prom

Chapter 14
Some Of Jon's Remarks

"Mom, I have a new friend. She's cute. She works at the C.D. shop. I like her. She's blonde. I set her up to fail."

"Mom, here's how you get to the store. You go down Main Street until you turn right or left."

"Mom, I didn't want the McDonalds coupons for $20. I wanted $20. Then I could go eat at McDonalds and have the money on my stereo."

Jon with medals from Special Olympics

Chapter 15

Clutter...Clutter

Ben threw down his cap on entering his room. But, when he'd entered the front door, he'd thrown his communication book in the corner. His lunch-box made it in another corner. His bedroom was neat, when he'd left for work, because I had supervised his getting it all put away. Within ten minutes after he came home, his music tapes were scattered around the room, his jacket on the floor, and he had taken off his white socks and walked on them as he stumbled over his boom box. He was constantly reminded to "please put your dirty clothes in the basket,", as I walked each step along with him. "let's put your tapes in the boxes", I said. "Ya", he said with a question mark look as if it didn't register, which it probably did not. The minute I'd leave his sight, he was cluttering again.

However frustrating this may seem, we must never stop repeating, remain calm, patient and understanding. Those words that the Pediatrician had said about Jon, "And he can't help it", comes to mind. Sometimes we've made simple lists with pictures to help him remember. You do what works even though it may seem hopeless. Each tiny accomplishment is a time for praise, praise and more praise. Whenever I say, "good job...well done", his eyes light up and he'll holler "Ya!" Yet, I may know that no one reward, or praise, or celebration has lasted until next time. So, we begin again at square one. We will and we will always look for a glimpse of success, sometime, some day...maybe?

Both sons' rooms were clean one moment and the next became a disaster. They never remember where they put anything and they throw things down wherever they happen to be, no matter how many reminders are given. Both are destructive of their belongings at times, as well as those of others. Keeping their rooms small and with as little as possible in them works best as they never can find what they need.

Ben enjoying a cool dip in the pool

Chapter 16

The Other Sons

I've wondered, at times, what these two sons would have been like had alcohol not been fed to them prenatal, before they could be the ones to choose. Would they be married with children? Would they have homes and cars and jobs? Would they be able to enjoy the lives that my biological sons have enjoyed? Perhaps, they would have graduated from college or vocational school. I probably would never have known them then, and I would have missed out on a lot of the joys, the humor, the rewards of knowing and parenting these special young men.

Alcoholism is, at the beginning, a choice. It becomes, for many, an addiction. When a woman makes the choice it is her life. But, when she becomes pregnant, it becomes another persons' life. That happened to two of our sons' lives. They will journey through their lives struggling each day in a world of confusion that did not have to be. My heart aches for them. They had no choice.

The "Other" Boy

As I look upon his questioning face, when I try to explain what to do while he runs around, confused and lost in his thoughts and dreams, its true that although he's a man, he's only a boy, searching for pleasure each step of the way. Living for the moment, not even a day. As I think of the car he will never drive, and the freedom he'll never see, it tugs at my heart for it is true. It's a child he will always be.

Chapter 17
The Problem

Jon and Ben are the two young men that have come into my life when they were very young, so I have known the peaks and valleys of their growing up. Of course, they differ from others with F.A.S., as they, in ways, differ from each other. Since they were children, I have met other children who have similar problems, some who are diagnosed with F.A.S. or F.A.E.; some probably even more who are not, but by knowing the history of their birth mother, and seeing the children, it isn't difficult to see what they problem is.

It would, however, be difficult to tell a birth mother that her child or children's conditions were caused by her alcohol drinking. Some mothers may be unaware of this and it would be very hard for them to accept. Others may be so far into their addiction that they couldn't leave the alcohol alone during their pregnancy, even though they knew that it could cause these problems to their unborn child, and they are in total denial. Whatever may be the case, it is a vicious circle in cases where the children are able to make choices in later teenage or adult years. They too will very likely choose to drink alcoholic beverages.

There seems to be an inherited craving in these people. Even for Jon, who has F.A.S., and cannot choose to drink. He has that craving and he has asked me if he can have beer several time, even in his teens. With guardianship, of course, I will not approve. With the severity of his F.A.S., even the excess candy affected him. Someday, I hope, society will find a way to prevent what now still is allowed and no child will have to be born with this preventable disability. Because this is such a sensitive subject, and because it affects free choice, it has long been un-addressed by those who could make laws. Because of my closeness to the situation, I remain very concerned as well as speaking out to young people every chance I get. Many young women have listened attentively and asked questions such as, "When during pregnancy does it affect the baby?" Also, "How many drinks are allowed?" Or, "Does alcohol always hurt the baby?" To these questions, I can truthfully reply, "It is unknown." Then the question that I hope they will remember, "Is it worth it to gamble with your precious baby's lifetime for your short-lived immediate high?"

You have a choice, and this may be the most important choice you will ever make for you and your child. If you choose to drink, your choice is for not only yourself. I hope that you make the right choice. If not, you may have to live with the guilt the rest of your life, while your child lives in a world of confusion as well as probably health – (both mental and physical) problems. He may have problems making friends, and probably poorly choosing any friends he may make. He may make many mistakes over and over, because he doesn't learn that there are consequences for behavior. Perhaps, he will have seizures, or a heart condition, eye problems, or a mental handicap. He may even be in prison some day. He may never bond to anyone his entire lifetime. He or she is the innocent one. As Jon stated to me several times, "I wish I was normal. I wish I didn't have F.A.S. I wish my (birth) mom didn't drink." How can anyone hear these words and not have tears in their eyes? It isn't something I can change by kissing it away, as I would the other "owies" he had, like when he fell off of his bike and skinned his knee, or when he got sick with a fever. Its not like there's an antibiotic or a surgery or a "rest in bed" that can take care of it in a short time. It's there, forever, and I'm helpless.

As for Ben, he is unaware that he is any different from anyone else. He is very happy and content the way he is. He has never asked any questions about his birth parents, nor has he mentioned the word, "alcohol", to my knowledge. His world is complete with what ever he does. Eating is his favorite joy and he says that every food is "good mom". He is luckier (in this respect) than Jon. Ben has no concept of why anyone is different. He does believe that everyone is his friend most of the time, although he does have his favorite people. One employer gives him a soda and he's one of Ben's favorites. Anyone who he enjoys being with, he will say, "he's my friend, Mom." Although he will complain about anyone who doesn't please him for one reason or another.

Ben at Special Olympics

Ben holding Lassie

Chapter 18

Crises

One day, when Jon was home, the individual who was helping take care of him was watching him as he was spinning in his unique pattern, round and round, with his music. Jon, suddenly, looked at her and threatened her. The look in his eyes meant that he was serious. After several phone calls, that we made, police arrived and cuffed him. He seemed not to even see them, yet he said, "I'm not going to resist." The ambulance arrived soon afterwards and he was transported to our hospital, where he was given a shot of Haldol to calm him. The on-call Doctor asked me what I wanted him to do, and I explained that he needed to be taken to the larger city where he could be observed and he could have a medication change, if needed. For a week, he was observed and his medications were adjusted. Then, he went back to the group home.

Another time, he attempted to hurt a vulnerable person, and had to be restrained. At that time, I was in the way and I got hurt. The scar on my arm is the result of a nail injury that took fifteen stitches to close. He has ever since been very remorseful. He remembers part of it. I always tell him that is in the past. He says, "Ya."

He was sent to another facility about two hundred miles away one cold February because of severe behaviors. He spent two months there and we drove down there and visited him several times. We wrote letters and sent packages. It seemed so far away, even though he also called us almost every day.

Chapter 19
The Hyperactivity Problem

Jon was hyperactive from the moment I met him. He bounced around here and there non-stop. It seemed a miracle that he didn't end up in the emergency room a dozen times a day. Yet, he never had a broken arm, nor any cuts and bruises. The more exercise he got, the better. He excelled in swimming, running and tumbling. Despite the fact that he was legally blind, and wore the thickest lenses I'd ever seen, his coordination was exceptional. His long, thin fingers and toes could clutch like claws around the wooden beams in our living room ceiling, while he'd climb across the room, grinning, and if he saw me looking frightened, he would laugh. He loved the attention which Ben loves too, even now in their twenties. They have always liked to be the center of attention. I've heard of a lot of others with F.A.S. that are the same in this respect. They attract the attention of others in school, work, or the community, because of their being socially inappropriate. They do not have to try to be noticed at all. It is natural for them.

Jon loves babies

Chapter 20
The Important Ingredient

Both Ben and Jon feel good about themselves, most of the time. There are times, however, when Jon seems sad and withdrawn, but it is because he is reaching for the unattainable man that could have been. It is at those brief times that I hurt for him. But, I must accept what I cannot change.

Then, there is Ben. This sweet young man loves life and he loves himself. His excitement at whatever comes into view is contagious to all around him. Self-esteem is so very important.

Ben next to famous sculpture

Chapter 21

Schools

We enrolled both of our sons with F.A.S. in elementary school when they came to our home. There were some problems, but the school had not dealt with someone like Jon before, so it was a learning experience for them as well. Although they never told us that it was our parenting, we believe that may have been what they thought. At one of Jon's meetings after he had been hospitalized at the University of Minnesota, and had just returned to school, the teachers and especially the principal started bringing up all of Jon's worst behaviors. I said, "Stop! Before we go on, let's talk about Jon's strengths. We all know about the problems he's been having." I explained about the new medications that he was started on and that it could be another week or two before they took full affect, and that the problems he had were complicated by the fact that he was in puberty.

Negative remarks have no place in school team meetings. What we can all do to help the child succeed is what is of utmost importance. If we do not keep this in mind, we would be setting him up for failure. We cannot allow that to happen. I asked the superintendent to send Jon's teachers to a workshop about F.A.S. I also attended this workshop. I hoped that by them hearing about this specific disability, they would know first of all that it was brain damage, and that he was not willingly misbehaving, as well as getting some ideas of how to manage and help him.

Jon was home-schooled for a short while when his behaviors became too severe for the local public school to handle. A behavioral analyst came to our school and our home to observe Jon in different environments. The last time that he came to our home, Jon locked the door so he couldn't leave, not because he wanted him here, but Jon wanted to make his times here to be over, and he felt that if he made the man upset, the next time he wouldn't come. Jon never wanted changes in our home and to this day, he wants everything in our home to remain unchanged.

When it was decided that this school wasn't the best place for Jon, he started in a school in the city where he still lives. We had explained beforehand what worked and what didn't work to the school officials. They didn't listen and decided that they were the professionals, not the parents, and that they would do things their way. Their way didn't work with Jon. He destroyed some equipment in their library and we were sent the bill. However, we learned that we were not responsible, because they had refused to listen to our experiences. After this, things improved as time went on, for the most part. We did have our problems, at times, all throughout his high school until he graduated. He had two very dedicated teachers there who helped a lot. We wanted him to learn to the best of his ability the life skills that he would need most. I've often thought that he should have been in an acting school. He is a great imitator.

Jon was call "a pioneer in the field" by a Superintendent of a local school. He had a time out room, but I doubted that he understood why, nor did he remember the next time that he was put there. Ritalin, we soon learned, wasn't the answer. At school, as at home, we learned that what worked for others didn't work for him. Rewards helped, but only until he had the reward, or more often, destroyed it.

Ben had few problems in school. He does have a very sly way of taking objects that are not his and that is how he got in trouble occasionally. One time, he patted a girl on the behind when she walked by him outside of his classroom. The teacher asked him, "why" he did that. His reply was, "she's cute." We had no other problems that were significant, except for a short attention span, which is expected with his disability. I believe that his diagnosis of Down Syndrome, beside his F.A.S., has made him more quiet and mellow.

Of course, there are all sorts of differences in people. When one is known to have F.A.S. / F.A.E., one must not overlook that there may be other factors involved in this person's make up. We, for example, do not know anything about Jon's birth mother, except that she was an alcoholic at a very young age. We know nothing of any other problems she may have had genetically.

We do know that Ben has a lot of relatives with diabetes, common also in his Native American heritage. We have him screened for this each year and watch for symptoms. Other than the fact that the birth mother also abused alcohol, we know very little. We wonder at times if our sons birth mothers are even living, being the sons are both now adults. Often times, the birth mothers are deceased by the time their sons or daughters are teenagers, because of liver problems from the alcohol addiction. Most do not live to raise their children to adulthood if they raise them at all. Without help for the mother's addiction, she is most often unable to care for a child, especially a child with the special problems hers may have. The child may then suffer from neglect or even abuse. There needs to be help for these mothers and their child or children with various services if this is to be successful. When some mothers learn what caused their child's disability, they will accept help for themselves and therefore be able to help their child. However, I believe this is usually not the case. The mother may mean well, but alone cannot help herself.

Chapter 22

Foods

Why Jon has always craved a bitter tasting beverage amazes me. He has at times drunk a whole bottle of pure lemon juice, down in a matter of seconds. Another time, while everyone was eating a meal, he went in the kitchen and consumed the entire family's dessert, a peach cake with cool whip on the top. Jalapeno peppers are also a favorite, straight from the garden.

Ben enjoys any food and seems not to have any strange tastes. Like many people, he loves chocolate. His birthday barely is over when he begins to ask about his next birthday, and he always says, "chocolate cake!"

Probably, neither Ben or Jon's cravings are due to their having F.A.S. This is just mentioned to show that this population is still more like everyone else than they are different. They have many of the same basic needs, desires, and dreams as others without F.A.S. / F.A.E. do. They, of course, need help to get their daily living skills done, to learn to do whatever they can independently, with supervision and to try to accept what can never be reality.

One of Jon's most endearing traits is his way with an older sister who is a lady with both Down Syndrome and who has autistic tendencies as well as obsessive compulsive disorders. Both live in the same city and ride the same bus to the Developmental Achievement Center to work. Jon sits by his sister and he says that he "takes care of her." He tells me that she will hug him and being somewhat nonverbal, to a great degree, will still say a word or two to Jon. It is very touching, the interaction of caring between two people raised as siblings with different types of disabilities. Both were adopted from states thousands of miles apart, brought together as, what we believe, was all in God's plan. We believe that he sent these two to the same city so that Jon could be there for his sister on that bus, and at their place of work. Tonight, in his sweet voice, Jon explained how he had helped his sister that very day on the bus. I told him how very proud I am of him and how important he is. He asked me, "Mom…do you thing that I am ignorant or funny?" I told him that he was very special, that he was not ignorant. I told him that in what is most important in life, he is very intelligent, because he cares and helps his sister and that he loves the Lord and each of his family. He said, "I love you", as he often does. I know that he means it. It is a gift that I cherish most of all when each of my children tells me that they love me. It is these moments when I feel "recharged", ready for whatever comes next.

Ben enjoying a warm summer day

Chapter 23
The Future

All around the country, we see many, many young people, especially being irresponsible as they "party", drinking alcohol and having sex. We who know of these consequences feel that we are going to have a huge number of children with F.A.S. / F.A.E. and other drug addicted babies. If society chooses to ignore this, it will only increase as each year passes. Society as a whole will pay a price that they may not realize yet. The children will pay the biggest price, because they are the innocents. However, the cost to the government will be out of control. There is a tremendous cost to society for all of the special needs that these children have. So many are born prematurely, so they need intensive care, some for many months. With their health problems, they usually need many doctor calls, hospital stays, medications, and surgeries. They are more likely to need special school services throughout their school years. Some, like our Jon, need mental health evaluations and/or hospitalizations. They need foster care or group homes or other special living arrangements with staff for their entire lifetimes. They may need to pay court costs and attorneys fees, which means society is usually who pays, as they probably can't hold down a paying job that makes them self-sufficient.

Many people believe that the alcohol industry should be responsible for these high costs. There have been inquiries into this possibility and there will be more, I believe, as this population grows more rapidly.

Let there always be, first of all, the individuals with F.A.S. / F.A.E. and their needs being met before money is disbursed to pay for anything unneeded. Excellent staff and excellent teachers, for example, should be given the best wages, not the same as those who are in it for the money only. Priority should be given to the individuals' health and safety. Those, who care for these people, need to have their eyes and ears open so as not to overlook health problems in those that cannot or may not verbalize when something bothers them. Jon, for example, never dressed for the weather. He didn't put on his winter coat or hat or gloves, unless he was constantly reminded. It always helps to have an extra set of cold weather clothing also because of the person's inability to remember where he or she left their belongings. It is difficult to look up a missing cap, for example, when the clock reads 8:00 and at 8:01 the bus pulls up (been there-done that)!

Communication between home and school or work needs to be open at all times. A spiral notebook works well. Their name on the outside helps. I've gotten other children's books at home and our son's were somewhere else!

The future may give us parents and staff more clever ideas, as I've only mentioned a few. Most are just plain old common sense, but as parents and or guardians, we need to keep on top of what is happening by keeping eyes and ears open and good relationships with all who touch in any way our loved one's lives. We must speak up if we don't agree with what is happening, and praise those who show that they care about what is happening in our family members' lives. Together, we can do our best to ensure that these children and adults can live happier, healthier and fuller lives, to the best of their abilities. I can guarantee you will not have a dull moment, we certainly haven't!

Whenever Jon does not get his way, he still has what I call a temper tantrum. He always wants something new (and expensive) or something that we cannot agree on, in his case. He is very manipulative. His, still, most used words are, "I want." Sometimes, we can let him have what he wants, if it is affordable and something that is practical for him. But, many times, he cannot have what he wants, and at those times, I am very much the villain. He can be rude, and say things that I know he doesn't mean. Then, later on, he regrets it, feels guilty, and apologizes. It hurts me at the time, but I know it is his temporary reaction and it won't last. It is so like a two or three year old when he's told, "no more cookies right now." But, he is twenty-four years old. Probably, he'll be this "child", no matter how old he becomes. He grasps for the unattainable "object", but he's really grasping for the unattainable "man." If someone tells him "maybe", sometime later, such as at your next meeting, next year, or even tomorrow, he hears only "maybe", and to him, "maybe" means "right now". He hears what he wants to hear. This is sometimes also true of Ben. Although, Ben's birthday may have been a month ago, he has asked me for his chocolate birthday cake again, because every day should be his birthday. It is much less intense, however, with Ben. He will go on from this moment where Jon is "stuck" in a rut until there is something that replaces it. The cycle, then, starts over again.

Ben riding train

Chapter 24

The System

Our two sons with F.A.S. are on waivers. This gives them services which the state offers to the developmentally delayed, as they are called. "Case Managers" through the county of residence manage these services. There is a Social Security program call SSI that provides a set amount for those who meet the qualifications. There are "providers" who have staff that can help the person in or out of the home, depending on the person's unique needs and the wishes of the family or guardians. There is respite care for some people. The person along with the case manager "screens" the person to establish which and how much services can be provided. Families may decide if they want services and may decide if the staff available is acceptable for their family member's wants and needs. There should be goals that are worked on which the person receiving services needs to become more independent. The person's culture, such as Ben's Native American heritage should be always kept in mind when planning activities. Jon's swimming skills should be priority during the long summer days.

The work experience is hard to address, especially in rural areas for there are not many choices where larger cities have more chances for employment. The DAC's are where most of the mentally challenged youth in our area go after school years are over. Some of these people go out in the community with staff called "job coaches" with them to do jobs that they are capable of in places of business. Many others remain "in house" and do various jobs, such as shredding paper, cleaning, inserting flyers in newspapers, rug making and various other jobs that the DAC can obtain contracts for. They are transported to work and home after work. They take their lunch and once a month they are allowed to order out, which is something that makes Ben's day. Jon's DAC is much larger and it does not offer this opportunity. In Jon's DAC, there is not enough work to keep everyone employed. The future may bring better options for these people with disabilities. Concerned parents and guardians are working with legislatures as an ongoing goal.

Ben with D.A.C. group

Ben's Graduation Day

Ben in back row with hat off

Jon's Graduation party

Chapter 25
Needs

PREVENTION
IDENTIFICATION
EARLY INTERVENTION
STABLE ENVIRONMENT
DEDICATED CAREGIVERS
SPECIAL TEACHERS
EDUCATED STAFF
HEALTH NEEDS
PROTECTION
SAFETY
JOBS

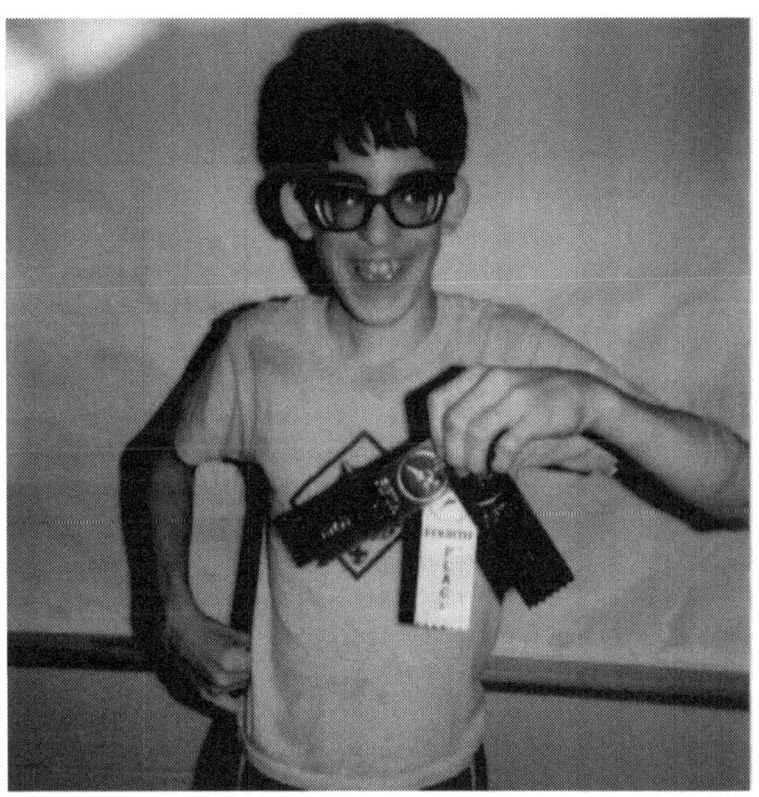

Jon with more medals

Chapter 26

Facts / Thoughts / Observations

1. F.A.S. is a brain injury due to prenatal alcohol exposure.
2. Some people with F.A.S. have normal intelligence, while the average IQ is 68. Some are lower. IQ is not usually a way to measure this population's intelligence.
3. F.A.S. is 100% preventable and 100% incurable.
4. A diagnosis is very important. It can help protect the child from being blamed for what they cannot control. It also can help you get needed services.
5. People with F.A.S. often confuse fantasy with reality.
6. People with F.A.S. may have strengths in some areas, but little or no strength in others.
7. Some days these people may do well and the next day do poorly on the same assignment.
8. The person's memory may be inconsistent.
9. In different environments, a person with F.A.S. may not associate that they must behave the same way socially.
10. Everyone is a "friend". There are no strangers. Thus – <u>very</u> vulnerable.
11. Socially, these people often act inappropriately. For example: One son, when six years old, asked a lady who was obviously very pregnant, "where do babies come from?" That may sound cute from a little child, but later when he asked a seventeen-year-old high school senior, she called it "sexual harassment."
12. Hyperactivity is very common. One son flits from one thing to the next like a butterfly, while the other son is much less active.
13. These children do best with lots of structure / routine.
14. One son spun round and round in a pattern – spinning to the music. When told he would be moving to a group home, he spun and twirled constantly. When I asked him "why?", his reply was, "Mom, that's the way my world is going right now." He was sixteen years old at the time.
15. They may go into "overload" if over-stimulated.
16. Many of these people are very sensitive and notice other folks looking at them, hear words said about them, etc. Respect them and their feelings. They may not hear it like it is said.
17. Many people who are "alcohol affected" love music. Both of our sons are great fans of country music. Our sons have met several of these stars personally.

18. Our sons, amongst others, are very compassionate and caring. One example was when Jon saw a house burn where two small children had perished in the fire. He told the father that he'd give him everything he owned if it would help, but that he knew it wouldn't help. This was very touching to the father. Both sons pray for family and others who are sick or have some other difficult time. They both will tell you they know Jesus.

19. Many people who have been affected by prenatal alcohol end up in the justice system.

20. Many children of alcoholics are raised by grand parents, other relatives, and adoptive or foster parents.

21. When a woman uses alcohol when pregnant, it is like playing Russian Roulette with her unborn child.

22. It is still unknown whether alcoholic fathers contribute to a baby being born with F.A.S. or F.A.E. Years ago, I met a person who, I believe, had F.A.S. and was told that his father was an alcoholic, but his mother never used alcohol. Research is being done on a father's involvement, if any.

23. It helps a caregiver to have a good sense of humor. Also helpful is networking with other caregivers. I have attended workshops and read articles from other parents experiencing problems similar to ours. Talking to other parents, one on one, has helped me to see that we are not alone and that it isn't our parenting that is wrong, it is the fact that our sons were born brain damaged and that they, more often than not, have very similar problems.

24. Each person is unique and yet I've seen more similarities within this population, in general, than differences. Of course, genetics are also important. One of our sons is a Caucasian and the other is native American. F.A.S. & F.A.E has no respect for the race or intelligence of parents. It is totally due to the mother's drinking alcohol while pregnant.

25. In Bible days, mothers were told not to drink wine or strong drink when carrying a baby.

26. There can be other diagnoses as well as F.A.S. / F.A.E. that these young people can have. A.D.H.D. (attention deficit hyperactivity disorder), conduct disorder, and autism are several of these.

27. Many of these youth are defiant in situations that have someone in authority. It could be a parent, teacher, or a Judge.

28. They usually cannot understand consequences.

29. In some, there is depression, even suicide.

30. Arithmetic is difficult for these people to comprehend.

Chapter 27
Helpful Hints

By direct contact with children and young adults with F.A.S. / F.A.E. I have my own opinions (that may not always be those of others) about how to deal with these folks.

1. Keep structure and routine as much as possible.
2. An environment that is quiet or has relaxing music helps.
3. People with F.A.S./F.A.E. need protection by parents, teachers, and staff, to keep them out of trouble. This may mean close "shadowing".
4. Do not expect them to remember tomorrow what they learned today. Tomorrow, to them, may mean "right now".
5. Do not set them up to fail by having unreal expectations of them. Help them to succeed by much consistent praise, not punishment.
6. Get as early a diagnosis as possible so that all of the help available for them can be begun early.
7. Laugh with them, not at them.
8. Remember how vulnerable they are. Do not expect them to understand this.
9. Remember that they hear "bits and pieces" of what is said. One son, when in school, came home one day and told me (matter of factly), "Mom...we're going to have intercourse at school tomorrow!" I was in shock, but his teacher explained what was said was, "we are having mini-courses at school tomorrow". At other times, they may say what they want you to believe. One son has "selective hearing", also.
10. Some medications may help with severe behavioral issues, but most do not usually respond to medications. If the people are caring for themselves, they probably won't remember to take their "meds". Our son who is medicated has trained staff to administer his meds.
11. Choose your care providers or "staff" carefully. If your family member is also considered "mentally challenged", he or she may be in a group facility. It is wise, then, for parents to become guardians, so that they can have active parts in decision making.
12. Accept your child, adult, or client. Look at their creativeness and cultivate them. Some are very talented in arts, writing, acting, etc. When one cultivates these talents and the F.A.S. / F.A.E. person's interests, you should see less "behaviors".
13. If counseling is needed, find a counselor that understands the "uniqueness" of people with F.A.S/F.A.E.

14. Parents or "staff" need to choose knowledgeable, understanding professional help for their sons, daughters or clients with F.A.S. / F.A.E.

Chapter 28

On Having Pets

When Jon was only six years old, soon after he had become adjusted to our family, we bought a pet black rabbit for him and the other children. We caught Jon hitting the rabbit so we couldn't keep it. We thought perhaps he was too young mentally anyway for a pet.

When he was about 13 or 14 he wanted a dog. We thought about it seriously and finally decided to let the children get a larger type puppy. Jon stood beside a litter of about a dozen puppies that needed a home. One of the puppies came rubbing up to Jon, licking him when Jon held him. "This one, Mom!" Jon said. "This one loves me!" So it was that the puppy he named "Coco" became a part of our family. We told Jon that it was his dog because he was the most interested in Coco. He helped feed and water Coco, walk him with a leash, and play with him. But as time went on, Jon spent less and less time with Coco and he no longer was willing to help with Coco's needs. This was typical of Jon. He lost interest quickly in every thing, especially if any work was involved. Yet, when Jon moved to the group home, he wanted Coco to go along. The rules where he moved to did not allow for a dog to live there, and we believe that Jon would soon have neglected Coco when the newness wore off, as it had at home. We noticed that Jon still played with Coco when he had his home visits and he usually asked about the dog when he called home. Ben was never as interested in pets as Jon. He does play with animals now and then, however. Sometimes people with F.A.S. seem to have a tendency to be cruel to animals so they should be supervised when playing with them so that the person and the animal will be safe.

Jon recently brought me a note from one of his DAC staff. It said that Jon had fun playing with her five-month-old son and that he had the baby smiling. Jon and Ben both seem to enjoy babies and younger children. Here again, they are always supervised. The foster home that Ben was a part of before we adopted him had reported that Ben had to be watched around the babies, and that was a reason that they decided not to adopt him as they originally had planned on doing. We never had that problem, but of course we were always with him and supervised him, when he was near the little children. He has been kind and the kids seem to enjoy it having him play games with them. Ben has a kind nature as does Jon.

When Jon was about 12 years old he took the goldfish for a bath with him in the bathtub and he sincerely thought that this was a necessity, but of course, the poor fish didn't survive and Jon felt terribly sad for some days about what was meant to be helpful, but turned out to be a disaster, and another learning experience for him.

There has been never a dull moment at our house as you can see. I know of no one who has spent any more anxious hours in doctor's clinics or hospitals. We have been very fortunate to have my sister close by who has taken over the rest of the family when we couldn't be there because of crisis. She and her two daughters were a real Godsend when one of our daughters had open-heart surgery and another had leg surgery, and when Jon had neck surgery for Torticollis, plus other sicknesses, etc.

In most homes there are crisis time when outside help is needed. You soon learn at these times which people you know are the jewels, as they will be there for you while others cannot or are unwilling. A cousin new deceased wrote to me once years ago and said if we lived closer she'd come and help, too. She had foster children who had health needs. She had been there. I'm sure that those of us who have had children all know how nice it is if you can get away once in a while to get a breath of air ourselves! For us, we never asked for respite. One lady said once, "You adopted them, you can take care of them!" That was a cruel, hurting statement. Another person, an attorney who helped us with our will was so different in his way of looking at it. He said "Look at all the money you have saved the government by adopting children with special needs." We didn't do it for what people think of us. We certainly have never been "paid" materially – our rewards have been in each tiny accomplishment we have seen in one of the children or adults we adopted. Other people who adopt these children will say "Amen" to this, anyway those we have known over the years.

As a parent of children with special needs I have been nearly physically attacked myself by two teachers at different times because I was standing up for the rights that the law provides for these and all children in public schools. Both were men. One was a head of a Special Education Department in Jon's school who was angry and threatened to "kick Jon out of school" if we took the matter at stake to a disability lawyer if it could not be resolved at school. He came towards me (I was sitting opposite him at a conference table. The matter later had to involve a disability attorney from the State who came to the next meeting and let this man know that he must go by the law to ensure Jon's rights were done by stating the law. I never saw this man again but heard son after that he was no longer at this school.

The other time was at a different school for a different family member with an altogether different set of problems and a different disability. It was a male member of the "Teacher's Union" who also came across the table as if to hit me. The school superintendent then yelled at this man to "Stop!" My husband on one side of me, and our private attorney on the other side were both ready to "take care of the situation had it gone any farther. Does this show that some professional people need anger management classes? I believed it shows that something in their education is sorely missing as well as what most little boys learn from their fathers

72

that "boys don't hurt girls", and these grown men showed that they have no control so how can they be hired to work with any child, let alone children who may be challenging to teach? Here again, patience and self-control in ones self is needed first. I have myself never been disrespectful to even these people no matter how they treated me. They had no reason to lose control. All I have ever said was that my children's rights were to be protected and that we parents by law are a part of their I.E.P. team for our children with special needs. Most people in these positions are not like the two men I had the misfortune to know. One lady teacher did once state that she was the professional! She had also lost control over the telephone for no reason that I could figure out. Maybe I should give her the benefit of the doubt and think that she had PMS or a bad day or some other excuse. After all, we are all human. I was twice this teacher's age, so I felt she should have remembered to show a little respect to her elders, or don't parents teach their children this as ours did to us? I tried calmly to answer her but she said that <u>she</u> was doing the talking. Most of her conversation did not even concern my child.

Some of these experiences make me happy that my children are all now past school age. It means a much calmer life for us parents. Some of our school experiences were very pleasant, however, we wanted to get along with people as much as was possible but could often sense with some of them that we were "only" the parents and they "knew best." Talking with many sets of parents of special needs children we have learned sadly that this is not an isolated case in our area but has occurred all over the country, in many schools and many states. These problems have caused many hurtful moments for parents who are only trying to protect the rights of those children who have special needs that the law tries to help by making laws that children need and are entitled to receive in what they call a free and individualized education plan built by a team which includes parents. Who else could know their child's needs better than the ones who live with them, hear their voices, watch their accomplishments, and have the deep emotional involvement in their futures? No "degrees" can match these qualities. A parent's job is not an easy road without thoughtless people who feel superior to them. I could never condense a book to make up for hundreds of volumes of our experiences with our family and how F.A.S. has added its beauty to our lives. It has made us see how important it is to accept each person as a unique individual. It has made us more aware of how another person (a pregnant woman) can change her child's life if she abuses alcohol and how that child, in turn, can change other's worlds, as ours have been changed. It makes us want to do all we can to help spread the word to other girls before they get pregnant. We believe that every school should have a special program about this problem. It makes us less tolerant of problems that can change another's life forever. We got banners at one time showing how a baby drinks right along with the mother and that alcohol is not concentrated when it enters the child in the womb. We were allowed to put them on the school walls. I have also written letters to the editor about this condition, hopefully to reach someone who needs to hear what can occur in the womb when alcohol of any unknown amount reaches the unborn child. I try to do my part by talking about this situation whenever the opportunity arises. Many such opportunities have arose over these many years. As one pastor once was quoted as saying, "what is on one's heart is what comes out of their lips." Certainly he meant the Lord, but also I can relate to that statement in another way. My sons, Jon and Ben and the condition that has changed their lives as well as our lives forever. I like my friends, relatives, and acquaintances to think of my sons with F.A.S. first of all as young men. (NO LABELS) They are more like us than unlike us. The labels are there merely to get the needed services for them that help them reach their full potentials. We know that we cannot change them as they are individuals, created by God with unique personalities and genetic materials. Yet I want others to understand that none of these problems manifested in these men are any fault of theirs. We like to have them looked at kindly, but not to be talked down to as if they were children. Rather speak to them as they would to anyone else but perhaps a bit more slowly and with words they understand. For example, when I heart someone tell Ben to act appropriately I asked the person "Do you think Ben understands the meaning of the word 'appropriately'?" I believe the person hadn't even thought that Ben needed to hear this in a simpler way. We must not take for granted that these folks with F.A.S. understand the way we do. Both of the young men hear parts of the conversations and interpret these parts differently.

One lady who has part of a team for our son, Jon, made a statement that sounded like Jon was the only person with F.A.S. that ever had violent episodes. I knew how very unknowledgeable this lady was about the syndrome (and yet she was on his team, supposedly knowing about this population. I told her that I knew this statement she made was certainly not true. I hope she asked others if she didn't believe me being I was his mother.

One time at another meeting for Jon I was so frustrated I got up, nearly in tears and left the room rather than explode or become overly emotional in the presence of so many "professionals." My statement, as I left was merely "You just don't get it!" Sometimes I admit, I do get overly emotional listening to people who think they know so much but have very little one on one time spent with a person with F.A.S. or certainly do not reside with these people. Throughout the many years that I have attended these meetings, both at school and at group homes, I have often made comments that sometimes seem to fall on ears that do not hear. At one workshop which a friend and I attended along with some staff from one of the group homes, my friend and I noticed the unconcern amongst some of those staff and the interest others showed in the presentation. Interestingly these same staff that had showed interest at the workshop were the same staff that we felt were excellent working with our sons. Some people are cut out for this type of work naturally, it seems. Others don't belong in this field at all. Some of the group facilities are very good places. I've always said that the staff makes the place a good or not so good home. Staff are hired to be there for their "clients". In some cases visitors see staff sitting around watching television and their clients roaming, bored, without the help they need. In other cases, good staff are interacting, playing games with the clients or taking them for walks out in the community or whatever pleases their clients fancy. In my opinion, the wages staff receive should reflect on how well they perform these services. This incentive could lead to better staff and happier clients and less behavioral issues. Good staff are like gold. Their work is at times quite difficult. They need to be rewarded by appreciative guardians, parents, case managers, and employers with words at least that show their work does not go unnoticed. As parents and guardians we also appreciate those staff who see another staff person doing or saying things that are not right and who report it to their employer so that disciplinary action can be taken. This has happened in our family member's case a few times and we always write a note of appreciation to the person who reported the incident. We need people who advocate for these vulnerable ones. We also feel that random drug testing should be mandatory in places where people work with the vulnerable population.

We also believe that the alcohol industry should be held responsible for women who drink when they are pregnant and the child or children are affected. Society pays the financial costs of these affected ones. Our belief is that the responsibility should be where it originated from, of course these are our personal opinions, yet we know that we are not alone in these opinions.

We who are concerned about these issues must keep on writing to those who make the laws, and we must lobby for what we want to see done. Many of us believe that change the system that exists, and thus help our family members and others who have F.A.S.-F.A.E. and to prevent this most preventable birth defect. For myself, I am getting old, so I sincerely hope I will see these changes in my lifetime. Unless one has walked this walk, they can never know how hard it can be.

Good communication is so very important. We have attended every meeting that is important to our sons' life. We are trying to be alert to any sign that situations are not quite right. We listen to what the young men tell us and we feel we know them well enough to sort out what is true and what may not be true most of the time. Usually this turns out right. There have been times when we may have misjudged them but probably at least part of their statements were true. They can both be manipulative. There have been times when it has been difficult to figure it all out. For parents and guardians who are responsible for the well-being of our sons with F.A.S. we are living with these challenges and others day by day, year by year, we can only do what we can to the best of our ability. We pray for our family members and for their staff and we try to get to know their staff enough to get a gut feeling as to their abilities and their morals that could make an influence on our sons lives away from us. We have had our favorites, of course, as well as some who we question their ability. To some it is obvious that it is merely a job with a paycheck while many others are working for reasons besides the paycheck because they enjoy their job and the people that they work with. We believe that it helps to praise the staff when they do well, as well as our son who lives away from home. Criticism is never easy to give but many become necessary at times. My father always said that we should look for the good in people and I never forgot it. I trusted everyone until an incident at school with a teacher who I had trusted turned my trust into skepticism. It is hard to regain trust if one has betrayed your trust. Yet, I know that most of our staff and teachers can be trusted.

Chapter 29

Ben

Ben's obvious enjoyment when with his Dad is very special. When Ben lived away from home he always told staff that he wanted to go to the "Coast-to-Coast with Dad." This store was a place where the two of them enjoyed going to when his Dad needed something, and Ben always accompanied him there. The latest place they like to go together is fishing. When Ben catches a fish he's so very excited but at first he didn't want his Dad to clean the fish as he didn't want to "hurt" it. He's so tender hearted. If there is a dead animal on the road that had the misfortune of being hit by a car, Ben will always say that it is "so sad, so sad". He loved each critter in a way that most people don't think about. A pastor once told me that it would be a wonderful world if everyone was eager to go to church as Ben was. Whoever is sick or hurt he always says, "I pray for (and names the person) and then he will add, "I make a card." One time Ben and a staff were in a car accident and although both were taken to the hospital by ambulance, Ben's bruised chest from the seat belt was his only injury. He kept talking about this accident for months, even years. It made a traumatic impact on Ben. He wanted everyone we knew to go and look at the "sad, sad car!"

Chapter 30
All That Love Isn't Enough

Although love, unconditional no matter what, is a very, very important basic need of all people, certainly when your early life has been unstable, when you have been passed around from one home to another like a football never knowing which Mommy and Daddy you will be with next, love to these children is uncertain. Adopting these children whether with our children's disabilities or whether any child, I'm sure that this becomes a part of who they are. For myself, I cannot understand how big of an impact this can have. My being in a loving, stable home. As our sons with F.A.S. came to us with other families before us, it must have been very difficult.

The first day that Ben came home he seemed to wonder if he could or should hug us goodnight. I can only assume he was wondering, "How long will this stop off place last?"

Jon missed the other kids in his last foster home and he talked about the house he had lived in for many months as if it was next door. We did our best to make them feel comfortable and loved from the start. Bit by bit, day by day they bonded, adjusted and trusted us. Along with their own F.A.S., it was difficult for them probably much more than had they not had F.A.S.. Soon we learned that all of our love wasn't enough alone to help these little boys. We knew that without much structure in their lives they would be denied a basic need.

Chapter 31

Networking

If anything has been a big help to me it has been networking with other parents who, like ourselves, are dealing with the challenges and joys each day of raising our children with special needs. No one can know better than they who also deal with school issues (they all do!) with children who taunt our children, with IEP's, and even with (but rarely) some doctors, like the ENT who once said to us, "If the child won't hold still you can leave because I can't do anything!) This said after coming at the child with a long needle looking device and absolutely ignoring the fact that our child could see, hear, and was obviously frightened, as I would have also been.

Most doctors have been wonderful, caring and kind, and we can never thank them enough. Networking usually with people we seldom meet face to face, but by phone or letters or emails, makes us a large "family" with a special kind of bond. So we become there for each other in bad times as well as the good times, in crying and in laughter. We've shared our challenges, heartaches, triumphs. We all know that we are not alone on that "island." Our tears are their tears and their tears are ours. We have so many common interests. These friends have grown in number over the years and include people in many states. Most of their family members with F.A.S. have grown up like our sons and present with a new set of problems than when they were children. Now it is where they will live as adults, guardianship issues, finances, legal issues, etc. Along the way we have tried as unprofessionals to share what we have learned along the way with other parents, teachers and caregivers, etc. All of us are eager to help (and sympathize) with struggling younger or newer parents with children who have this condition. It is rewarding to try and save others what us "pioneers" as we've been called, have gone through. Everyone does things a little differently, for we are different from one another, yet there are certain things we can all learn from others who came before us to make our parenting more successful. We all make mistakes and we can all learn by these mistakes.

My friends have asked me how I'd handle a certain situation and I've asked them the same question. Then each of us decide and do the best we can. Some of us have days that all we need is a shoulder to cry on or a listening ear to say, "It will be okay. Take a deep breath," or "I love you and know what you're going through." One thing we do not every do is to criticize our friends for the way they decide to handle a situation but rather we accept their decisions for their particular situation for we know they will do what is best in their own way. We pray for one another and for their loved ones with F.A.S. and know that they also are praying for us. Some of us may never meet in person because of the distance involved. Yet we are as close as the phone or letter. We understand if we call that the other parent may be dealing with a behavior or be otherwise too busy to talk at the time. We understand that because we realize that we are all busy parents. Most of us have other family members as well as our children or young adults with F.A.S.. Most are also adoptive parents with large families with some others with disabilities of some kind, not always F.A.S.. Some are parents of children by adoption who are other races as is our Ben and a daughter of mixed races who has cerebral palsy. There are many reasons these families are similar to ours and have similar problems. We can understand each other's needs. There have been newsletters that connect parents with others, also. We have subscribed to several such newsletters through our many years of parenting. They help in many ways.

We take one day a time. Each day is new and full of promise, full of surprises. We share the good ones as well as those not so good!

At the time when we felt we had to place Jon out of our home (not out of our hearts), I do not know if I could have gotten through it without my friends. Some of them have had similar experiences. I felt so sad, so even full of guilt (for not being able to keep him home longer) and was any of it "My fault?" At night I'd wonder if he was all right and had we done all we could for him? I'm sure my friends had felt those same aches in their hearts as I had. But we go one with life and accept that we did do all we could and that it was no fault of ours, and that we gave him, as one psychiatrist put it, a real home life for many years. Oh, how that helped to hear those words from a psychiatrist! But even then, at the time my heart nearly burst with pain, especially because Jon didn't want to leave our home, and years later he still wants to live with us, and I still wish that he could and probably would myself say he could, except for my wise husband who looks beyond the heart to reality. How thankful I am that he is so strong. He looks beyond today and sees that it wouldn't work anymore as we are older and more vulnerable now and we could not keep up with this still hyperactive and sometimes violent young man whose childhood "Temper Tantrums" have changed into grown-up behaviors that he cannot control. Our friends have been through this that have parented children who are diagnosed with F.A.S. or other drug problems that the birth mother had. Ben has not had these outbursts and seems to accept our decisions much better. His happy, accepting nature makes it possible to keep him at home where he enjoys being as he and his Dad do many activities together. The biological mothers of our sons may struggle with their own problems of addiction. They may still have in their own way the babies that still must take second place, in many cases, to their addiction. This is a difficult and sad situation for so far, anyway, there seems to be no real answer. No law says she cannot keep her child or children unless, of course, there is proven neglect or abuse of the child. Some emotional damage is bound to occur in these cases, however subtle it may be. Most of us adoptive parents have little knowledge of the birth mother's lives after the child is removed from her or voluntarily relinquished by her. Though sometimes a mom will try and seek help for herself so that she may get her child back before the child is released for adoption and some succeed. Others are incapable or unwilling to give up their "habit" for their child. So many of these children are with relatives or foster care in limbo until they are freed for adoption and can become a part of a new family. Grandparents often raise their grandchildren with F.A.S.-F.A.E.. Some of these grandparents lovingly become second "parents" at an old age. You never know what another's reasons are unless you have walked in their shoes a mile, so this excludes myself, not because I'm too strong to resist temptation, but by the grace of God I was spared from the desire to want alcohol. My four grown biological sons do not have to live with F.A.S. or F.A.E. for which I am thankful.

I am sorry for you mothers who do not get a chance to enjoy the children you gave birth to. I wonder sometimes on Ben and Jon's birthdays if your tears spill as you think of the young men. I wonder if your heart aches because your son took second place to your addiction because you could not help but drink. I wonder if you had other children later on and how these children have done, if they also, have the syndrome. But we remember you most of all, and we hope that you have sought treatment for yourself and we wish you success, and we thank you for the gifts of life you gave us.

Chapter 32
About Birth Mothers Of Children With F.A.S.–
F.A.E.

I am not here to judge you, condemn, nor to make you feel guilty. Had it not been for two of you, unknown to me, we had not had the two beautiful and loving sons who you birthed. I'm sure you must have hurt deeply when you forever terminated your parental rights to your babies, not knowing who would be their parents. I know that the disease of alcoholism is so strong that it has overcame many lives. In his records from the agency we learned that Ben's birth relatives have diabetes in their history. This is common in Native American people, we learned. We have Ben checked for this at each yearly physical and are on the lookout for any signs of this disease in Ben. Should Ben get diabetes it would be very difficult for him as his biggest joy has always been food. With each meal he always says, "Supper's good, Mom!" no matter which meal it is. It makes my day. He is a very appreciative person for whatever is done for him He is so full of life and has such a happy disposition. So often his over friendliness is not appreciated by people who do not understand him. He will always be someone who you meet and can't forget. He seems to know more people in several communities than we do and he greets them all whether in the stores or on the street corners. I often hear someone holler, "Hi Ben!" He gets so excited, waves his hands up and hollers back.

Jon was very small when he was born. Ben wasn't much larger, although both were full term pregnancies. This is consistent with many babies born with this condition. Jon has long, thin fingers and toes. At birth he was Tactile Defensive. A specialized medical foster mother spent much time encouraging him to eat as he grew. His early pictures showed a very cute little boy with a big smile. We weren't as fortunate to have baby pictures of Ben. However, when he was several years old, we saw also a cute little boy of Native American descent. These pictures are treasures to us, as are the records that were provided by agencies. Jon's eyesight is not good. The optometrist said that Jon's retinas look like those of an elderly person's. He wears very thick lenses and is considered as legally blind. He needs frequent blood tests for liver and kidney functions because of the medications he has to take to control his behaviors. Psychiatrists see him on a regular basis to monitor his medications if needed, to check his blood work, and to visit with him and staff. If things do not seem as they should be we have also attended, as we have over the years, other doctor appointments. The specialists once told us that when young adults get in their twenties they may become more mellow and less hyperactive. Jon's hyperactivity has carried on in his twenties. Like a butterfly he sometimes is quiet for a short span of time if something truly interests him.

Otherwise he is moving around looking in to everything and touching, exploring, tasting, smelling many things. He knows that he is allergic to nuts and he can tell at first taste if there are nuts or peanut butter in a cookie or other food and he will ask about it or tell people if the food contains anything with nuts in. One time at school the cook accidentally gave him a cookie and he suddenly had a severe reaction which frightened everyone around. We make sure that allergies are noted on all their records for whoever may work with them. It is Jon's records as Ben hasn't had any reactions to any that he so far has had. However, he could not eat breads or anything with gluten when he was young. It was felt that he may have celiac disease but as he grew older it was not found to be a problem. We always know if Ben has any pain and Jon h as gotten better to tell staff. They both used to tell me and I had to relay to staff. I kept explaining to them that I am not there so I cannot help them. They need to tell whoever is with them, staff being available. This has been on ongoing concern. Jon called me at midnight once saying he was having a hart time breathing because he had been with a staff who was smoking and Jon is allergic to smoke. I asked to talk to the fellow in charge who said he did not know that Jon had allergies and he was unsure of what to do. I told him "call 911 and get him to the hospital!" He did and Jon again was told, "You must tell staff when anything is wrong, when you don't feel well or have an allergic reaction. Once when Jon was at a temporary center for behavioral problems, we drove several hundred miles to se him and when we arrived, the first time I looked at him I saw an orange colored thick discharge coming from his ear and running down his cheek. Getting closer I smelled a terrible odor. "Jon," I said, "Have you told anyone about your ear?" "No" he said, unconcerned, just obviously happy to see us. I asked to see the nurse who no one had mentioned this to before. It should have been very obvious to anyone who was near him whether he told them or not! Had this happened at home it would certainly be called neglect. There seems to be a different standard for these places than there are for parents. I've heard this from many other parents with similar experiences. Parents know their children so well that they can sense if the child isn't well. It shows in their eyes and in their behavior prior to other more obvious symptoms. When we entrust our precious sons or daughters to another's care, we need to expect that their health and safety are foremost.

Chapter 33
One Of Jon's Letters

This letter is from someone who wanted to learn about F.A.S. and the doctor's response:

Dear Doctor _____: I hope you can help me with some information about alcohol use during pregnancy. What is the chance that two or three drinking binges (four to eight drinks) during the second trimester have caused brain damage. I am overcome with guilt over my stupidity. Anonymous.

Answer: Fetal alcohol syndrome is a preventable tragedy if pregnant women abstain from any amount of alcohol throughout the entire pregnancy. The likelihood that fetal alcohol syndrome will occur depends on the amount of alcohol drunk, the duration of its use and the time of pregnancy at which it was drunk. Many experts feel that the most critical period is in the early part of the first three months of pregnancy. However, no one has defined with certitude any safe amount of alcohol at any safe time during the pregnancy. When a pregnant woman exposes the fetus to alcohol, fetal development is slowed. The baby is often underweight at birth and might never attain normal height and weight. Various facial abnormalities can occur. A fold of skin can cover the inside corner of the eye. The jaw is often undersized and the upper lip quite thin. Brain growth often lags, and the child can have learning disabilities that remain for life. Heart anomalies can occur. Holes can appear in the wall that separates the right and left sides of the heart. I wish I could give you the assurance you want. I cannot. Your use of alcohol was limited, so the outlook is not entirely glum. Thank you for telling your story. Your candor and anguish are strong deterrents to other women who might be tempted to drink while they are pregnant.

One Of Jon's Letters

Hello, my name is _____. I have Fetal Alcohol Syndrome and was adopted by a nice family named the _____. I like to listen to Country Music and I know Pam Tillis. I was put in REM in 1994. I had some problems with behaviors, but now I have changed. I go to school in ____ at the high school. I have a very nice teacher named Rhonda. I would like to move back to _____ and live on my own in an apartment. I'm very independent and very smart. I have four other brothers. I think they would like to see me grow up.

This picture is of a normal brain.

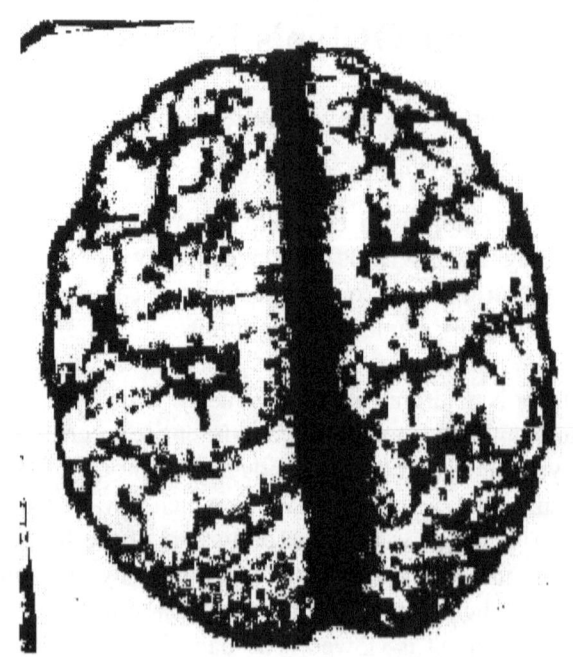

This picture is of a F.A.S. Brain.

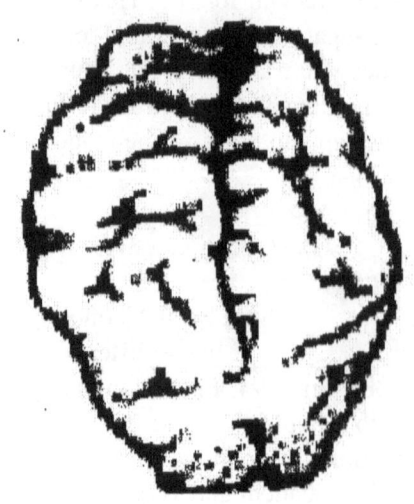

Chapter 34
Letters

Another thing that could really hurt is when anyone looks at the parent as if it is certainly their parenting that made their child behave in such a way. Sometimes a parent even can hear this, sometimes it is just sensed. But you must look beyond these remarks and keep doing all you can for your child because you would be wasting precious time if you let others who probably don't even know the reason for the behaviors get your attention. Think otherwise of the knowledgeable doctors, psychologists, psychiatrists, and others who are respectful of you and your way of parenting a very challenging child. I would like to share some of the letters in the pages ahead from caring professional people.

January 29, 1992

Dear Mr. and Mrs. _____,

I appreciated meeting you when you brought _____ to see us at the University of _____. I am hopeful that the care by Dr. _____ on a new trial of medicine will be helpful for _____'s condition. I was certainly impressed by your loving care of _____ and realized what a severe stress his condition is for you. The plan of networking with other parents with F.A.S. is certainly an important part of your life. You should also feel willing to contact the public health nurse in your area if you have special needs.

I look forward to seeing you again if you come back to the University for follow up. I am tracking down your concern about how to teach _____ about his sexuality. At this point I would be aware of his sexuality issues and would probably deal with him in a matter of fact way. One technique I might suggest is when he raises questions about sex is to reinforce your love of him. It is obvious from my experience with other children that they need to be reassured that they will be loved and cared for by nurturing adults.

Sincerely,

Robert W. ten Bensel, MD, MPH
Professor, Public Health and Pediatrics

Fetal Alcohol

Dear Ms. _____ :

Thank you for contacting me regarding mandatory random drug testing for staff who work with vulnerable adults in group homes. I appreciate the opportunity to respond this issue.

I, too, am very concerned about seeing that vulnerable individual living in residential programs receive safe, high quality care. I will share with you some information about the status of current laws regarding random drug testing. ___ Rules, Part 9543.1020, subpart 14 requires programs licensed by the Department of Human Services (DHS) to have a policy that prohibits employees from being under the influence of a controlled substance when responsible for persons served by the program.

_____ like most other states gives employers broad discretion over setting drug testing policies. (The exceptions include a handful of states where laws actually prohibit private employers form conducting random drug testing on workers." ____181.951, subdivision 4, permits but does not require, employers to perform random drug tests on staff in "safety-sensitive positions." A safety-sensitive position includes on in which drug or alcohol impairment could threaten the health or safety of any person. DHS interprets the law to permit group homes and other residential programs to conduct mandatory random drug testing on employees. With exception of certain government workers and employees in the transportation industries, random drug testing is not mandatory under federal law.

A state law to require mandatory random drug testing would likely be challenged on the grounds that it violates a person's right to privacy under the _____ Constitution. While the outcome of such a suit is unknown, in previous rulings the _____ Supreme Court have found that the _____ __ Constitution provides for stronger protection of privacy rights than the U.S. Constitution.

I share your concern about protecting the safety of vulnerable individuals living in residential programs. I will certainly give your concerns careful consideration as the Legislature considers legislation during the 2002 session.

Thank you again for contacting me regarding this matter. I appreciate having your advice on this matter.

Sincerely,

Ted_____
State Representative

PARENTS' PERSPECTIVE

We decided against the recommendation of the doctors, which was to place our fourteen- year-old (then thirteen) son in residential treatment. We brought him home because one caring psychiatrist said that he felt, "home – a stable, loving home – is the best thing for him." Our son was born with fetal alcohol syndrome. He has a deep bond with us and us to him. He has been our son for nine years.

We feel his medications and a personal care attendant have helped us so much. His education still remains a problem. He cannot attend regular classes, and so far can go only one hour a day to a vocational class where he enjoys making objects out of wood.

Our community and our school are not set up to accommodate our children with such conditions. I wish that they could understand what parents go through to appreciate what parents need. I feel frustrated at the meetings, which seem to all lead to dead ends. I feel that parents are the ones who best know the needs of the child. Parents should be given the authority to make the decisions on what best will help the child and themselves and there should be providers for those services. The services should be community-based, and should be found not *only* in cities hundreds of miles from the child's home – when this happens, parent-child relationships become strained.

We *live* with the child. The professionals read and study but this doesn't mean they understand because most professionals have never lived with these children 24 hours a day, 365 days a year. Put the power in parents' hands. Let them do what is right for their child and the child will be best served, happier and healthier.

Submitted by Irene_____

December 30, 1991

Dear Mr. and Mrs. _____ :

Thank you for contacting me regarding the problems that you have been having with your son with Fetal Alcohol Syndrome. Unfortunately, experience does not support any specific type of drug as a "cure" for aggressive behavior or temper outburst during adolescence in F.A.S. children. They are worth a try under close medical supervision.

The temper outbursts are well documented in the literature. As adolescents they may get into difficulties in making judgments with friends, picking a wrong crowd, and aggressive behavior. One article goes so far as to say that "all have trouble with the judicial system."

Since society and professionals are just beginning to address these issues, I would suggest that you not close your mind to other alternative approaches rather than only drugs. What is needed is a coordinated effort between the educational system, mental health system, medical care, and support for the family. At the present time these services are not fully developed in any part of the country that I know of. I do know that Services for Children with Handicaps (_____ ___ Department of Health) is exploring a way of diagnosing and is attempting to develop resource services for children who are afflicted with Fetal Alcohol Syndrome.

There are many other conditions which are easy to prevent but difficult to treat. On the other hand I have seen children who have done remarkably well with a coordinated service approach. I would suggest you contact Dr. Pi-Nian Chang (U. of M. Psychology Clinic) who provides psychological and mental health services to these children. One of the questions he would want to know is whether or not the child has had psychological testing and would probably request a review of these records. I would also be happy to see your son and see what the other services we might be able to identify to help you and your family as well as your son in this most trying time.

I will be back in the office on January 6 and look forward to hearing from you.

Sincerely,

Robert W. ten Bensel, MD, MPH
Professor, Public Health and Pediatrics

May 8, 1998

Dear Ms._____:

On behalf of the planning committee for the "Just the F.A.C.T.S." workshops on fetal alcohol syndrome, we would like to thank you for your presentation. The Depth and Variety of knowledge offered by the presenters was apparent at each of the workshops. Participants gave the workshops very favorable evaluations.

Altogether, 537 people attended the workshops, which were held in _____. You have contributed to a greater statewide understanding of how to address F.A.S. and other alcohol-related effects.

Best wishes to each of you, and again thanks.

Sincerely,

Doreen Kloehn
F.A.S. Research Analyst
_____ Department of Health

Debbykay Peterson
Early Childhood and Family Initiative Specialist
_____ Department of Children Families and Learning

Genie Potosky
Child and Teen Checkups Coordinator
_____ Department of Human Services

Fetal Alcohol

Dear Irene,

Thank you for writing and for letting me know that you would like the legislature to consider a law providing for mandatory random drug testing of employees who work with vulnerable adults.

You mentioned in your letter that you have a personal reason for making this request. Perhaps it would be possible to share your story with me at some time. I can assure you that anything you tell me will be held in the strictest confidence.

I intend to discuss his issue at some point with the Chair of the Senate Judiciary Committee, which oversees privacy issues, in order to get her perspective about whether our current state law could be expanded.

Thanks once again for sharing your opinion with me on this important issue.

Sincerely,

Senator Jim_____

November 24, 1992

Dear Mrs. _____:

    Thank you for your nice letter of November 13, 1992. I continue to be amazed at how well _____ is doing. If I can interpret the picture correctly he seems like he is becoming more and more adjusted from all the love and care you are providing for him.

    In regards to _____ whose pictures you sent me I can not make a complete evaluation from the picture. The fact that the mother was an alcoholic is important information. From the photographs I would say he does not have Down Syndrome.

    I would need additional information. The records you have sent to me for review indicate that he weighed 6 pounds 15 ounces at birth. I do not see a length. Generally, the data is quite specific that many of the babies have failure of weight gain. The size of the head and intelligence are important as they are established in the first trimester when the mother was using alcohol.

    It is also consistent that he didn't take solids well and didn't suck on the bottle very well. The other data obtained in the birth records are normal routine tests and are normal. The diagnosis of Down Syndrome is not made by x-rays of the pelvis but by chromosomal analyses. You could make an appointment for him to be seen at one of the Children with Special Disabilities Clinics provided by the _____ Department of Health. You could arrange such an appointment through the public health nurse in your area (probably a contact in _____).

    Obviously some of the signs of Down Syndrome can overlap with F.A.S.. It is easier to rule out the Down Syndrome with a chromosomal test and evaluation. The additional information that I would need are included on the enclosed sheet which we use in the F.A.S. clinic. How tall is _____ now? How much does he weigh? What's his head size? He wears glasses and it would be helpful to know what his eyesight is at the present time. How are his teeth? Does he have trouble with the enamel on his teeth? Are his teeth coming in crooked?

    I would perceive (based on his close-up facial picture) that he does have a smooth philtrum. The upper lip is difficult for me to judge. Without seeing him in person it is a very difficult judgment to make on the basis of a photograph alone. Certainly the history of drinking is important during the pregnancy which may explain some of his mental problems. We know that F.A.E. (fetal alcohol effects) may be a result of early drinking during pregnancy.

    If you bring _____ back here to the hospital to see the psychiatrist you could bring _____ along and I could take a look at him.

Sincerely yours,

Robert W. ten Bensel, MD, MPH
January 4, 1995

Dear Mrs. _____:

Thank you for your letter. Yes, I have discussed your son, _____, with Dr. ten Bensel and I have read your letters to him. The experience you are having with _____ from my reading of the literature is not different than other parents are experiencing with their F.A.S. teenage sons. Even with the best possible interventions early in life, the outcome seems to be very consistent, i.e., much out-of-control behavior in the adolescent years. We don't know whether that is peculiar to adolescents or whether that will be something seen throughout the life span. There are many questions that are unknown and treatment is mostly guesswork or borrowed from other conditions that share some similarities with F.A.S..

If I may make some comments about his current treatment, he is on Lithobid which has a known antiaggression effect, on clonidine which has been useful in attention deficit disorder which these children often have, and Haldol which also has an antiaggressive effect. You should consult with his psychiatrist to discuss changes or adjustments in these medications. You might consider the use of resperidol up to 6 mg per day rather than Haldol. The resperidol is not thought to have the long-term side effects that Haldol does and it may be more useful in conditions where emotional lability is a problem.

I agree with you that he should be maintained in the community at all costs. You speak as though there is a plan to take him out of the community. I don't understand why that should be. If he continues to be aggressive at school and at the group home and therefore is not suitable for those placements based on judgments made by the group home or school, then a program that specifically deals with his aggression that protects staff and protects your son should be implemented. A Rule 40 is the usual mechanism for this and some consistency between the group home, his family home, and school would be very helpful. You should ask your case manager to intervene in these settings in order to effect a consistent program.

Thank you again for your interest in consulting with me. There are certain needs that these children have which are not being met because of a lack of understanding of the mechanism of the problem and money for research. A registry of all the children with this condition in the state and a parent's therapeutic support group would be a useful first step. A parent's advocacy organization for children with F.A.S. in _____ would be helpful. I know you are a very active person with lots of energy. You might consider directing your energy into these three goals in order to help _____ and other children like him.

Sincerely,

George M. Realmuto, M.D.
Associate Professor

Dr. ten Bensel was one of the kindest doctors and people that I have ever had the privilege of knowing. He called me at home to discuss Jon at lengths and I certainly could sense his real concern. He was never judgmental and he did his best to lead us to whatever paths of help during our crisis during Jon's puberty. He asked our permission to use Jon's picture in an article about F.A.S. that he was preparing. The article that this was in is the following. It was a teaching paper for younger doctors to learn from. He was the first doctor to tell us that Jon had "full-blown F.A.S.."

Robert ten Bensel, posed by a slide of a boy with full-blown FAS, points out some of the typical features of such children: a flattened midface, thin upper lip, rotated ears, small head, and short eye openings.

We know nothing of Jon or Ben's grandparents or other extended biological families and little of the biological parents. Some of our friends have even had a birth mom be adopted by them before the child was born and later the child who she proved incapable of caring for, even with all of the kind help that they gave her. Those were tough times and we shared them with the adoptive family by telephone. I'm sure that we collectively could write volumes of our experiences raising our children with F.A.S.-F.A.E..

The first doctor, Dr. Jewett, Jon saw after he became our son as the man who told me, after watching Jon a while, "and he can't help it!" Dr. Jewett was an intelligent, caring man also. I asked him if he could get me information about Jon's condition and he copied off pictures and information about F.A.S.-F.A.E. from his medical literature and even offered his help if we needed him to attend our school meetings.

Dr. Kaplan

Dr. Kaplan is a very special doctor also. He was very helpful to all of our family through tough times with his expertise in medicine and his kind encouragement. I can say that these three doctors were great as well as Dr. Becker, a psychiatrist and Dr. Bahnson, also a psychiatrist. All of these doctors never were judgmental of our parenting.

As one psychiatrist wrote of him, the closest resemblance of normalcy he could have, we hope that you have prayed for him as we have and do. And yes, he has been told about his first mother in gentle words about how you loved him, too, but that at the time you were unable to care for his needs so you did what you felt was best for both of you by giving him up for adoption.

These young men have worlds of their own where they are the King, the Master of their Destinies. Ben was described to us before we met him as a "survivor." Some of the past sometimes comes back to haunt him. He recalls a "daddy with a beard" at times who was unkind to him. We learned that a picture of this man that Ben brought along seemed to frighten him. Another child from his past he missed for a while. As time wore on he mentioned these people less. There is the F.A.S. but it is also the past memories that make Ben the man he is today. It is like all of us, a mixture of ingredients from our genetics, our experiences of the past that make us who we are. Each of us are products of our past and our present. For our two sons that are alcohol affected the brain was altered from what it would have or could have been. This part of their being has changed but in many ways they are the same. I often wonder how many people in the general population are walking around with some part of them different than they would have been had their mother not used alcohol.

Perhaps, I've thought, you light a candle on a little cake each birthday of the son you had, and think of him, as we do of you. And we wonder if you are alive yet, for so many alcoholics die before their child becomes a teenager.

If you are alive and if you wonder, we'd like you to know that we have done our best to raise your son the way I believe you would have like, and we have loved him the way you would have, had things been different. We want you to know that he has had love.

Ben And Jon's Words

This book would not be complete without words from the mouths of Jon and Ben, the young men about what this story is all about. One of Jon's staff typed the story as Jon told it. Ben told me the words for his story. Both men are very honest and sincere, and their stories describe them very well. They "tell it as it is". We are happy to know that in their own words the reader will see that the Christian values they learned at home are a real part of their adult lives. Prayer is a big part in their lives. The concern for each family member shows that bonding of people who are not biological siblings can be very, very real. "Family" means so much to each one as it does to us, their parents. We have never had material wealth but in what is most important, family, we have the richest gold.

Ben's Story As Told To Mom

My name is _____. I like to walk with my Dad. I like to ride bike with my Dad. I like to eat at Subway with my Dad. I like to fish at the lake with my Dad. I like to go shopping with my Dad. I like to go to church with my Dad. I like to go places with my Dad. I work at a DAC. I cut shredding papers with scissors. I shred papers. I wash tables. I go to Post Office on Friday to clean and I mop the floor. I vacuum. I go to _____ on Monday. I put cookies on a shelf. I smash pop cans at work. I clean bathrooms at work. I clean windows on the door. I eat lunch at DAC. I help walk to Precious. Precious is our big van that takes me to work. I like work.

We have a puppy named Roxie. Sometimes he sleeps by me and licks my face. He is white. He wags his tail. I give Roxie food.

I pray to God that Cheri Lyn will get better, and I pray for Mom and Dad. Cheri Lyn is my little sister. I pray for my sisters and brother. I pray Mike's back gets better. He is my boss at DAC. I read at work. I work on a computer.

I like hot country music. I like Billy Ray Cyrus. I like Tricia Yearwood. "I'm in Love With that Boy" and Shania Twain to sing "I Like a Woman." I like Highway 101. I like Nintendo 64. I like a fish game and a boat racing game. I go to People's First meetings. We eat Pizza. I like sausage and hamburger pizzas. I take lunch to DAC.

My glasses were bent. I got them fixed. My pockets get checked. Sometimes I take things that aren't mine at work. I like water at work, not pop. The doctor said no more pop, drink lots of cool ice water.

I went on a trip to Black Hills. I was happy. I rode a brown horse. I sleep in a motel. I like to camp. I make marshmallows and graham crackers with a stick. They taste good. I like to sleep in a tent to camp. In summer I go to Bible Camp on a lake. We go in a big boat. We play games. We sing songs. We pray in chapel.

We eat, we have fun at camp. We had meat loaf, mashed potatoes and gravy. I am happy. I have friends at camp. One friend is Dave. One friend is Paul.

I like to go see my uncle Archie. He gives me cookies. My mom cooks supper. It is good. I like fish. I like rice. I like hot dish and chili and soup. I love to eat. Mom says I am good. I like to work with letters with my brother. We eat out at Burger King or Taco John's sometimes with friends. We have fun. When my brother comes home on Sunday we play.

I got my check. I can buy tapes. I can order out. On Friday 31 I order out at Subway. I like chicken sandwich. I like God. I pray Cheri Lyn get better. I like the stars and moon and sun. I take my Mom to door to show her moon at night. My Mom like moon, too. She say "pretty moon." I like Indian powwows. I dance there. My girlfriend dance with me. I like feather head bands. I get a cross to wear at powwow. I get the mail. I watch for cars on street. My hair is black. I like white new shoes. I like Christmas shirt Mom and Dad give me. I like Indian belt buckle for birthday. I like new games. Christmas is lots of fun. Lots of family come home. We get presents. We eat pizzas, turkey, ham. Mom makes candy, cookies, lots of good food. I like movies, and popcorn. I like UNO and cards and dice. I like snow to make a snowman and slide on a sled. My bike I like. I am happy. I have brothers and sisters. Cheri Lyn is sick.

Jon's Story

My name is _____. I was born in Portland, Oregon. My mother was drinking when she had me. I have a syndrome that is called Fetal Alcohol Syndrome. I as in two foster homes before I came to the _____. I have five brothers and five sisters. I've been having lots of problems since I've been five. I've been placed in lots of hospitals. I moved to REM _____ in 1994, and in 1998 I moved to REM Alan. I used to go fishing with my dad; we had lots of good times. I used to have my mom cook. I had two dogs. I really hated it when Cheri Lyn had her surgery.

I got in trouble a lot at school. I used to do things that were bad. I used to tear up students' papers. I wish my mom would come and see me. My mom is someplace in the world, but I can't find her. It's really hard some days to go day by day without thinking something's going to happen. I think that it might rain on me just because I did something wrong. But I understand why my mother left me. I'm living here in a world where everyone thinks everything's going to be all right.

My mom's name is _____. See, I went to Nashville in 1995. I had fun there and got to see Pam Tillis. Pam Tillis came to _____, and I got to see her. I got a picture of her, and I got her autograph. I have another dream: I want to move to the Cities. I like the Cities because it's a lot like Nashville. I've been behaving really well these days. I wish I could keep my spirits up and go ahead in the world and get a better job, but it's really hard to find a job when you're not like the others. People look at you when you're different. That's how I feel. I wish I was in a spot in the world where I could just spin my lire away and there were no more worries anymore. But I realize I have all of this good stuff ahead of me, and I can't give it up.

My real mom does not know me. My foster dad does not know me. I feel really sad, you know. God makes us as we are, and we cannot change that. When the warm sun's on me, I think about all of the good stuff, and every time the phone rings I think it's my mom. Every time I send a letter to somebody, I wish I would get an answer back. My brothers and sisters love me, and I love them too. They always see a part of me that I cannot hide. I wish that my life could be turned around, everything could be solved; I could walk farther and talk less. Sometimes I look at myself and think, "Do I have the intelligence to go out with other people?" Sometimes I look in the mirror, and think that I'm a nobody, and I do everything wrong. My dad is very special.

My mom was born in 1968. She had four children, and then she got us. I used to win a Father's Day trophy for my dad. He thought that was pretty special. I used to go to school in _____. I had several teachers. Their names were _____ , _____, _____, and Jim _____. Terry _____ was my teacher in third grade. _____ was my teacher in second grade. _____ was my fifth grade teacher, and then _____ was, too. Then _____ was my special ed. Teacher. I used to like school very much. Now I'm graduated. I work at the DAC. I used to have Ronda _____ in high school. Then I had Jenny _____ as a helper. Then I had _____. Then I had Robby _____. I used to be in Special Olympics, and I got lots of medals. I used to work very hard at school. Sometimes I would have problems at school, and then Ronda moved away. Now my teacher is Deb _____. I used to have lots of classes at school. I used to take Home Ed., Small Engines, and a check writing class with Julie _____. The funnest part of the day was when we had to go to lunch at 11:30 a.m. On January 21st, Troy used to come to school, take me out of school, and teach me.

It's the year 2000 now and it's March 18. I'm going to have a meeting on the 29th of March. I'm going to discuss about how I feel, and where I want to go. Tim said that it's not going to happen, but I don't see why I can't move because I think it's a good thing. See, everybody will miss me because I'm such a good person. But I know I will find myself a better place to live, a better job, and a lot more money. See, Tim said that when I want something really bad, I can easily have it. So right now I want a new stereo. My mom does a lot of stuff for me. She sticks up for me, and she fights for my rights. Sometimes I think that I don't deserve that because in the past I have hurt her. I have thrown stuff at her, I have called her names, I have thrown a board at her with a nail that cut her open. That's just mean. I know that I can control it now, because I've been working really hard at it. I've tried to change my anger as far as I can go. I go and see Dr. _____ in _____ every six months. Now I go and see Dr. ____ in _____.

I wish I had a girl friend, but some things don't work out the way they should be. See, my sisters have dreams, my brothers have dreams, and I have dreams. I lost my uncle last month. It was very hard for me. I have a reinforcement program where I buy one CD a week. I used to call my mom every day til something happened. Now I call her Tuesday and Friday. Every time I go to _____, I like to go to Chi Chi's. Sometimes I hit the TGIF restaurant. We just got a new restaurant here in town. It's called AppleBee's. I am trying really hard to change my heart around so that I can go on with life as I wish. Sometimes I think that if I don't do good, people will think that I'm wrong. I have excellent staff, and Tim is pretty good. We're starting a new staff today.

The weather is pretty fine here. It's about 34 degrees. I went home last weekend, and went to Bingo yesterday. I do my work like I am supposed to, and I try really hard to listen to the staff. The staff tries to understand how I feel on some days, but sometimes I tell lies. It's sort of hard. I just got a new computer, and I enjoy it. I play on it a lot. I try to write stories on it. I have a dog name Coco. She likes me. My mom's name is _____. My Dad's name is _____. My family is very special because we all have needs and our lives are like a circle. Sometimes I think that we push ourselves too much, and I have friends on the outside world. But God said that we are all special in our ways, but for me it's like pulling on a drawer, taking out silverware, and setting the table. I realize that things have to get done about me. I have to change the way I look, I have to change the way I act, and I have to start treating people with respect. See, I realize that turning on a light bulb doesn't solve all your problems. And for me, to go on in life, we have to look at it as another picture.

My staff really like me in _____ but other people think I'm smart, and I am smart. I may have ten friends, but hey, that's just me! Sometimes I wish that I was something else, you know? I have a girl here whose name is Katie, by the way, she's typing this for me, and she may be a blonde or a brunette, but she's an angel. I tell a lot of jokes. Some jokes are nice, and some jokes are dizzy. I like to live in _____ but the green grass grows where the beans grow. What I'm trying to say is wherever you find the pot of gold is where you find the treasure.

There's a little story I've got to tell you: When I went swimming in _____ I used to be a good swimmer, and I used to take swimming lessons. But one day, I was riding my bike back home with a gal named Jan _____ and I had a little accident. My foot slipped off the pedal, and went into the front spoke of the bike, and flipped me 50 degrees over. And as I was headed head first for the ground, I was thinking, "Am I going to survive this fall?" At the time, I was not wearing a helmet. God must have been watching over me. One time I had to go into the hospital because I stuck a bead in my ear.

My life has been instrumented since the day I was born. A lot of people have come and gone in my life, and I have learned a lot since I've been a kid. See, I have a lot of allergies. I've been placed in many homes. But to be honest with you, I only remember half of the people that I saw. Someday, I'll be laying in a hospital bed barely breathing, barely speaking, and I'll wonder, "Is this the life that I want to live?" I want to live in a community with good air, good people, and good food. I realize that money doesn't grow on trees. And sometimes I think that my friends are not always there for me. I'm sitting here today talking to you about reality; how life goes on, how day goes to night, how minute goes to minute. But as I'm sitting here I think about all those people who are drinking, and how that drink affected me. I realize that alcohol is not good for your heart, but why do people do it?

People think drinking is cool. I heard some people say, "Oh yeah, we're going to get plowed tonight!", and to me that does not turn me on. Okay, lets think another reason: Why do people do drugs where these drugs could affect me? I realize people die by day by day. Maybe because of illness or a car accident or just by sudden death. See, people don't just live on this earth to throw out their arms and say, "OK, I can help you!" God put us on this earth to show respect, show interest in him. God wants us to grow up nice. God wants us to turn to Him and thank Him for all of the good things He does for us. See, people may think that people are people, but God thinks differently. God puts our souls in our bodies to live for Him. People may be driving cars these days, but some people don't have a car. Some people are living on the streets. Some people are digging in trash cans today for food. Well, I put three dollars and fifty cents into a container last night to help kids that are sick. I realize that people need love, but I can't provide that for everyone. Sometimes I think that I might open up a restaurant for people that don't have food and serve it to them for free. I know how people feel when they don't have money. They can't afford to buy food for the kids, they can't afford to pay the bills for the house, and some people take that money and go to the bar and drink. For me, that's not the way to go.

I wish there was a reason in the world for me to just go out. Why do you have to do this? See, a lot of people know ways that they can get a job. They can make money, but for me, I can't keep a job. I'm thinking that I can't keep a job is because I screwed up the first time. I never got a second chance. I wish I could buy things that I want to, but I realize that I have things to pay for first. It's hard for me to describe people when I se people on the streets pushing grocery carts full of clothes, and I see people wearing regular clothes. I wish I could cook for them, and say, "Come in, come in to God's house. The Lord is here to serve you!" I may be a handful, but at least I have a heart. I wish that people could stop drinking and doing drugs. I wish people would stop killing other people, and I wish that people who are in jail could change their hearts around, and pray to God, and have God forgive them. See, that's not the lifestyle that I want to be getting into. I wish that I could have a job where I can earn a nice decent paycheck, and go out and do things that I want to do. But sometimes I think that the walls are not always dry. I mean, I see some people looking good driving fancy cars and wearing nice clothes. I wish I could just cross my feet and relax, but as I stand here talking to you, I think, "Is this really getting through to you?" See, if I had it my way, I would give my life to the Lord. I would give my life to someone else who wouldn't have a life. Now, I am a nice human being who listens to country music and talks about gospel.

I have some friends who are pretty good. Their names are Mr. and Mrs. __ _____. Mrs. _____ cuts my hair, and she always talks to me about country music. Sometimes she gives me her magazines. I realize that I'm a special boy who has a big heart and talks to other people who need to be talked to. I wish one day when I die that I would have a copper casket. I've been deciding that I want more things to happen. I like my family because they are special to me, and I wish that they would act a little bit closer to me.

I have an uncle named Archie. He's getting up there in years. I went to Nashville in 1994. It was very fun. We got to go to the Opryland. My music means a lot to me. I wish that I could go to Nashville to do an album for Pam Tillis. See, Pam really likes me, and Pam said that if I needed a place to stay that she would put me up for the night. Pam Tillis has a son named Ben. I really like Patty Loveless. I talk to Patty Loveless sometimes when I se her. I asked her how things were going. She said fine. Then she invited me over for dinner one night. We had fried chicken and tator tot hot dish. And then she played *My Kind of Woman, My Kind of Man*.

I have more friends than I can count. But friendship does not have to go by anger. We all have a point in life where we must stand, and where I stand is where the flag stands. I'm proud to be an American, to roam free, to do what ever I feel like doing. I like _____, it has nice lakes. My dad cares about me. My mom cares about me, but sometimes I wonder what's going on with the world. How is the world turning. We will never know. I'm only one person who can work seven jobs out of five days a week, earning $28.50 a week. But at the spot light side by me, I think that it's time to where my feelings come to your feelings. I feel for you. If you get hurt, I'm there for you. If you have a meeting, I'm there for you. I will always be there to wipe away your tears. I'm a brother who takes care of business. I love my family dearly, but my moment away doesn't solve all of my problems. If a bird doesn't eat its food, find. A bird doesn't have to eat its food. If people are scolding me for something wrong, I believe I did something wrong. But God stands up to us and says, "Shall not fear; God is here!" See, I used to have an uncle, but he passed on, and he was a dear, sweet, intelligent guy I would ever meet. Not just because the way he looked. You could see it in his eyes. He had trust, he had beliefs. You know what? While he was on this earth, he did what God told him to do. Now since God said, "John, you've done all that you can do, time passes on." See, John loved his family. He loved his grandkids. Betty feels hurt because John passed over. Betty is my aunt, and I love her as much as I love anyone else. Not that I take her trust as loyalty. Poor Betty, she has been through so much that I feel for her. I know what she's going through. I know that she is hurt deep inside, but maybe I'm God. Maybe I can heal her. There's a thing in the world where loves comes to trust. In order to use that trust, you've got to earn it. Sometimes I lie to my people. Sometimes I protect the ones that I love. But the ones I love the most, I wonder, "Am I doing the right thing?" See, I'm giving my trust to a person who takes my trust and keeps it, and that's my family. My family takes their love and spreads it over the whole nation.

I got to tell you a little short story. One day it was sometime in February, and I was over at Jan _____'s house, and I couldn't go out because I did something wrong. Jan was doing the dishes. Jenny came running in, and said there was a fire over at the trailer court, and then a minute later the ambulance pager went off, and said all units had to respond. And all I remember is Jan saying to put my boots on. I had to run with her. It was some people's trailer that was burning up. I felt very bad for those people. I know how those people felt. But two little children burned up in that fire, and all I remember is I was sitting in a trailer and this mother came in with Jan. She was full of blood. Her hand looked cut up. She was crying, "Oh, my babies, oh, my babies!" and I felt very sad for her. So I went to the funeral home and saw them. I kneeled down to the mother. I grabbed her hand and said, "The Lord is taking care of them, they're going to be all right, they're in good hands." I said I would help her, I said I would give them my house. I would give them my love. She said yes, but she couldn't speak to me, but she couldn't say it because she only knew Spanish. He came up to me, patted me on the back, and said, "_____, you are a good man. You have a heart and soul and you care for us."

See, it doesn't matter who comes into my life, it matters who comes out of my life. I give my life to anyone who loves me. If I had a chance to save someone, I would give blood. But since I can't give blood, it doesn't matter. But it matters that I can be a better person. Sometimes I wonder what time it is some days. I wish that I could go home somedays from work. I have a couple people who I really like, who are at work. It's really hard to describe words when you can't spit them out. Sometimes I think that my parents are sitting right here; they're talking to me. God made me to be special. God told me that I have a job to do. He told the disciples that they had a job to do. God came down to me and said, "_____, what's up? I'm going to give you this job. How about you come down to earth and teach people about me?" I said, "Well, Lord, do you think that could be a challenge." He said, "_____, I know you can do it!" See, I try to be respectable, I try to be straight.

One day, when I was at _____, I got my head stuck into a toilet. I got mad, and I just sat there for a minute, and I thought, "God, what do you want me to do?" He came back to me and said, "_____, you got your head stuck in a toilet, don't you?" I said, "Yes, Lord." He said, "Go out there and tell them your head does not belong in a toilet." So, what I did is I went to the staff. My head was dripping wet. The lady at the desk said, "Who did that to you?" At the moment, I can't speak. She said to come out with her, and go to the living room and point to anyone who did that to me. I pointed to that person. That person got sent to the office, and I had to come along to be an eye witness. I got done, went to my room, and turned on my music.

I came back to _____. I was a little bit better, but I still had some problems to deal with. Not with staff, but with me. At that time, I had to use a method of STP. That stands for Stop, Think, and Plan. I usually like Christmas time. It's my favorite holiday. That's when family comes around, and that's when God's born. God came on this earth to take away our sins so someday when we die, we can go up to heaven and see Him. See, I can't control the way I think, but what I can control is the way I act. I can tell myself when I get into trouble that hey, back off, it's not worth the while. I have feelings deep inside me. The good feelings, the bad feelings. But some days I feel depressed. Some days I don't like this person. Some days I don't like the world. But see, I like animals, I like people, I like good humor, I like country music, I like making plans for the future, I like putting myself ahead of the game.

See, astronauts walked on the moon. But God walked on the water. Now for us people to walk on the water is pretty impossible! Being _____ is part of my job. I have to show people how they can respect other people, and to do that, I have to teach myself how to teach other people. Se, I like to be alone in my own little corner where I can just go off and dream. I like summer days when the days are warm. I used to like going to summer school. Sometimes I think that I'm just too short to do something just because people are tall enough to reach above my head. See, nighttime really gets me down, and it's almost like talking to a wall, but I always talk to myself because that's the only person willing to talk to you.

Well, I live in this house. I live with other people, and my parents say I have to live here. Maybe I'm better off being locked up someplace. See, I was going to do some room cleaning today. I was willing to clean up the house. Well, that's all I have to say, so good night!

For Ben And Jon
from Mom

They say that love's a mountain
So our mountain's very high.
We've shared the greatest moments
That reach up to the sky.

We've had our many challenges
Mixed with a lot of joys,
Since we chose you for our own dear sons
When you were little boys.

You've always been such treasures
Though life for you has been unfair.
You cheer us with your presence
That shows how much you care.

We ask the Lord to bless you
And keep you in His care.
We hope there will be many years
We'll live, and love, and share

To My Readers

In these pages, I have brought you into our home and our lives. I have shared some of our difficult times, as well as the happy times. I wanted you to get a glimpse of what it can be like parenting children with F.A.S., without a "recipe."

There was no set of directions that came with our sons. There are no right or wrong ways for every situation we face. I'm sure that there were situations that we could have handled better.

If anyone criticizes, so be it! Better yet, walk a mile in our shoes! We've done the best we could do to the best of our ability. What others think is not our problem.

Those first years living this experience we wandered alone on an island. But, we learned more and more that many others walked this path as well. Not all of their situations are the same as ours, but there are many similarities.

For the newest on this journey, I wish you much success. I wish you the joys of parenting that we have known. Then, most of all, I wish the mothers-to-be that hear our story to take heed. If you cannot quit using alcoholic beverages during pregnancy, please get help. Do it for the sake of your child, for his or her future. PLEASE!

Mom Irene

Post Script

Life goes on at our home and at Jon's group home. The day for us begins with prayer. We ask the Lord to watch over each of our loved ones and their staff. Yesterday was a hard day for Jon. He needed Haldol to calm him. Ben had ear problems. Both are better today. It is a new day today and it is a new beginning. Ben just looked at me and smiled. "Can I bowl tomorrow?" he asks with anticipation. "Yes Ben," I reply. We must take life one day at a time. Tomorrow is a question mark for those with Fetal Alcohol Syndrome or Effects.

Brothers at school

Brothers with little sister

www.ingramcontent.com/pod-product-compliance
Lightning Source LLC
Chambersburg PA
CBHW051437280526
45785CB00003B/1327